BranDesign®   BranDirection®   BranDream®   BranDiscovery®

DREAM IS AS IMPORTANT AS CREATIVITY!

BranD — International Brand Design Magazine

BranD

issue 19 FEB 2015

Published by
Sendpoints Publishing Co., Ltd.

Edited by
Editorial Department of BranD Magazine

Publisher
Gengli Lin

Chief Editor
Nicole Lo

Design Consultant & Art Director
Gary Tong

Design Director
Nicole Lo

Designer
Anying Chen

Design Assistant
Lexuan Li

Executive Editors
Lisha Xie
Sophia Li
Winny Xiao

Editorial Desk
editorial@brandmagazine.com.hk

Advertising Inquiries
Nicole Chen
+86-20-89095121-8023
ad@brandmagazine.com.hk

Collaboration Inquiries
Nicole Chen
+86-20-89095121-8009
marketing@brandmagazine.com.hk

Distribution Manager
Sissi Li
+86-20-89095121-8002
overseas01@sendpoints.cn

Address
Room C, 15/F Hua Chiao Commercial Centre,
678 Nathan Road, Mongkok, Kl, Hong Kong
Tel(HK): +852-69502452
Fax(HK): +852-35832448
Email: info@brandmagazine.com.hk

Website
www.brandmagazine.com.hk

ISSN
2226-6542

International Distributors

Mainland China
Sendpoints Books Co., Ltd.
+86-20-89095121-8007
zhangjuan@sendpoints.cn

Amsterdam
Athenaeum Boekhandel
T + 00 31 20 622 6248
F + 00 31 20 638 4901

Poland
Muzeum Sztuki Nowoczesnej
W Warszawie

Sweden
Papercut (Stockholm)
T + 0046 813 3574

Arnolfini Books
T + 0117 9172306
F + 0117 9172303

Artwords Bookshop [Rivington St]
T + 020 7729 2000
F + 020 7729 4400

Charlotte Street News
T + 020 7636 4270
F + 020 7419 7490

Corner House
T + 0161 200 1535
F + 0161 200 1504

Daily News
T + 7811155507

Fat Buddha Ltd
T + 0141 226 8972

Foyles
T + 020 7440 3265

Australia
Beautiful Pages
T: +61 401 55 55 36

New Zealand
Mag Nation (Auckland)
T + 64 21 366276
F + 64 9 3793096

Hong Kong
Foreign Press
T + 852 2756 8193

Macau
Macau Kengseng
T + 853 28522812
F + 853 28522813

Taiwan
Multi-Arts Corporation
T + 886 2 2505 2288
F + 886 2 2516 8366

Korea
Hong-ik Designbook
T + 82 2 333 0346
F + 82 2 333 0335

Japan
Azur Corporation
T + 81 3 3292 7601
F + 81 3 3292 7602

Malaysia/Thailand/Singapore/Indonesia
Basheer Graphic
T + 60 2 713 2236
F + 60 2 143 2236

India
SBD Subscription Services
T + 91 11 2871 4138
F + 91 11 2871 2268

Turkey
Alternatif Yayincilik San. Tic.
T + 90 21 2217 7363
F + 90 21 2217 7364

Chile
GONZALO OSORIO PETIT
T + 56 32 2397498
F + 56 32 2397498

UK
Central Books
T + 44(0)845 458 9925
F + 44(0)845 458 9912

Germany
Do You Readme?! GbR [Berlin]
T + 0049 30 695 49 695
F + 0049 30 695 49 696

Norway
Interpress Norge AS
T + 00 47 225 73241

Portugal
In Uteis Design LDA [Lisbon]
T + 00351 225 088 474
F + 00351 225 088 475

EUROPE ONLINE SUBSCRIPTIONS

Centralbooks
www.centralbooks.co.uk/acatalog

Newsstand
www.newsstand.co.uk

Contributions: We welcome all excellent relevant work contributions; however, we do reserve the right to select in accordance to different subject matters and quality purposes. All the works will be examined with respect and appreciation.

Fonts sponsored by Monotype.

Copyrights: All rights reserved. Reproduction in whole or in part without permission is strictly prohibited.

Editorial

Thanks for the gratefulness 2014 had brought, we had been gone through rebirth, searching for the meaning of exploration, sharing the fun of material design, and constantly narrating the possibilities in various creative fields for 365 days.

New mission lies ahead as we look forward in 2015. We are going to continue spreading brand design and creative positivity, sharing designs and stories all year round. Someone asked me why I insist on publishing brand design magazines? Certainly, I often ask myself what kind of media people need at the moment and what kind of information could impress the rush crowd? My answer is still very simple, it's the magical power, the positivity of BranD, I call it "dream". It helps people to understand design, to respect creativity and to realise one's dream.

In the year of 2015, we will have four brand new segments "BranDesign", "BranDirection", "BranDream" and "BranDiscovery". We hope this new version will allow a clearer future, an open content, which will boost designers to fulfill their dreams.

Branding, is often creating an emotional connection between brands and consumers through colours, images, materials and other visual elements. And if it touches human, it makes people feel fun and beautiful. What are those elements then?

"Positivity of brands" is what this issue about. Experience it with heart, appreciate the lively visual impression, and enjoy interesting stories that underneath, what it reveals is the answer.

Nicole.Lo

Nicole Lo
Exicutive Editor-in-Chief

Committee

Hong Kong Brands Association

Unit 605A, 6/F InnoCentre,
72 Tat Chee Avenue,
Kowloon Tong, Hong Kong
Tel   +852 2824 9328
Fax   +852 2824 9826

Hong Kong Design Centre

1/F InnoCentre,
72 Tat Chee Avenue,
Kowloon Tong, Hong Kong
Tel   +852 2522 8688
Fax   +852 2892 2621
Email   info@hkdesigncentre.org

www.hkdesigncentre.org

ico-D

455 Saint Antoine Ouest, Suite SS 10
Montréal, Québec
Canada H2Z 1J1
Tel   +1 514 448 4949 x 221
Fax   +1 514 448 4948
Email   info@ico-D.org

www.ico-D.org

iF International Forum Design GmbH

Bahnhofstrasse 8
30159 Hannover
Germany
Tel   +49 511 54224-0
Fax   +49 511 54224-100

ifdesign.de

Red Dot Design Award

Design Zentrum Nordrhein Westfalen
Gelsenkirchener Str. 181
45309 Essen
Germany
Tel   +49 201 30104-37
Fax   +49 201 30104-40
Email   team@red-dot.de

www.red-dot.org

Thailand Creative & Design Center

6th Fl. The Emporium Shopping Complex
622 Sukhumvit 24, Bangkok Thailand 10110
E-Mail: info@tcdc.or.th
Tel   +66 2 664 8448
Fax   +66 2 664 8458

www.tcdc.or.th

Shenzhen Graphic Design Association

Rm 1535, Shenzhen Sculpture Academy,
No.8 Zhongkang Road, Meilin, Futian District,
Shenzhen 518049, China
Tel   +86(0)755 8395 3338
Fax   +86(0)755 8395 3699
Email   info@sgda.cc

www.sgda.cc

German Design Council

Rat für Formgebung | German Design Council
Stiftung | Foundation
Messeturm, Friedrich-Ebert-Anlage 49
60327 Frankfurt am Main
Tel   +49 (0) 69 74748639
Fax   +49 (0) 69 74748619

www.german-design-council.de

Danish Design Association

Borsen, Slotsholmsgade 1, 1217
Copenhagen, Denmark
Tel   +45 72 25 54 00

www.danishdesignassociation.com

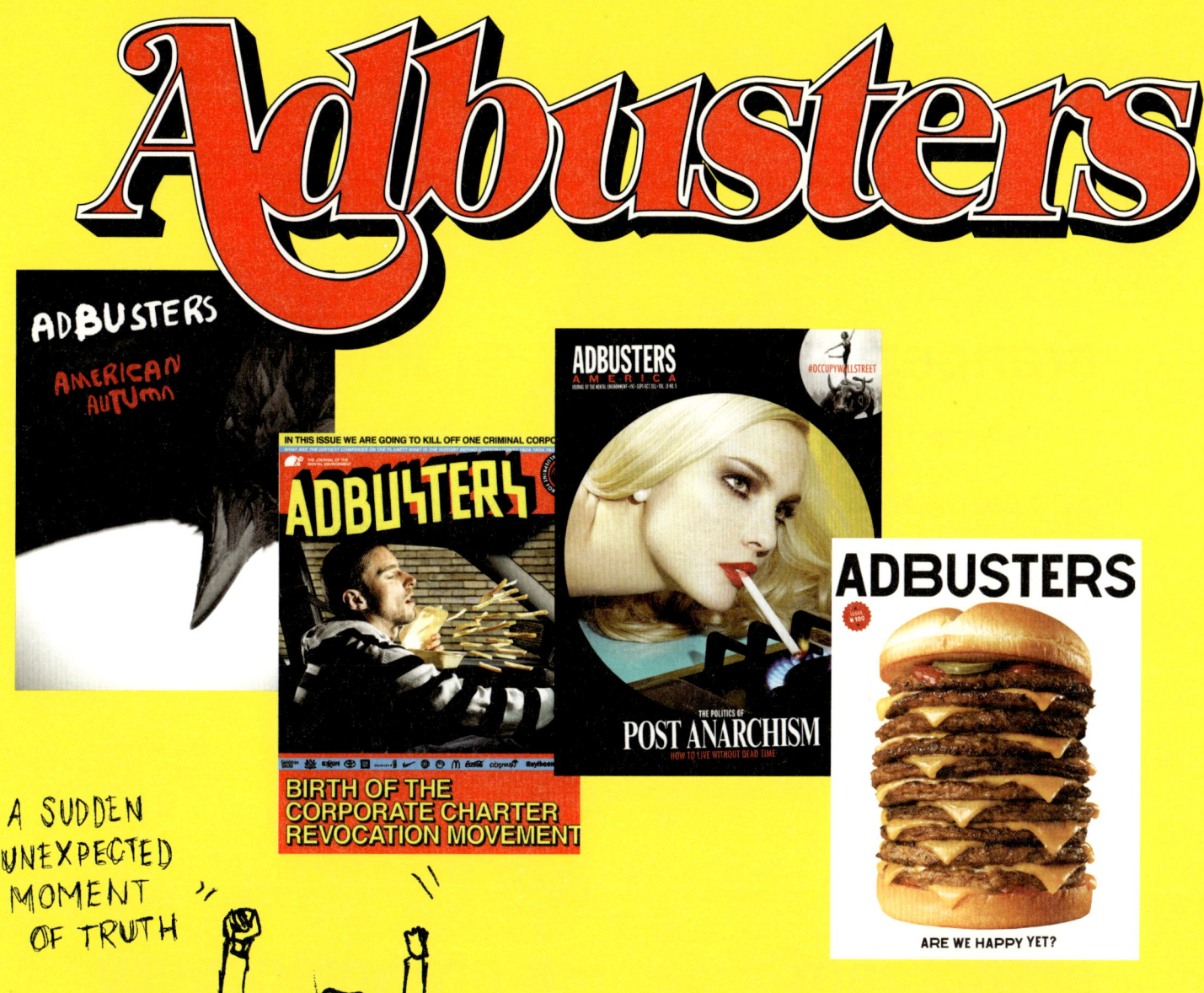

Adbusters magazine is the flagship publication of the global activist culture jammers' network. Known as the Journal of the Mental Environment, Adbusters has launched numerous groundbreaking cultural epiphanies into the noosphere including campaigns such as Buy Nothing Day, Digital Detox Week, Design Anarchy, and Meme Wars. In 2011, they sparked the #OccupyWallStreet movement with the original call for activists to occupy New York. Ad-free and operating out of Vancouver, Canada since 1989, it gathers writers, artists, designers, rabble-rousers, hackers, philosophers, pranksters, poets and punks who are changing the way information flows, shaking up the production of meaning in our societies, and dreaming of the first ever truly global revolution.

Subscribe here:
http://idnproshop.com/subscribe/adbusters/
http://www.idnworld.com/adbusters/

Contents

BRANDESIGN®

10 The Source of Positivity

56 Brands Love Kawaii

104 Creative Source from Food

BRANDIRECTION®

154 In Mobile Internet age, what is the core issue for Chinese brands?

158 Think Possitive, Make Possible

162 The Story of Brand Perfect®

BRANDREAM®

The Spirit of Hong Kong : Ambition and Creation

170 Passion Forging Your Dream

176 Crocheting the Family Dream

182 Mixing up Tradition with Innovation

188 Branding Hong Kong Culture

BRANDISCOVERY®

194 Originality

199 Events

200 Culture

GROUP SEX

----

ppaper SHOP

台北市中山北路二段26巷2號B1 | 02-2568-2928 | Tue.-Sun. 12:00-20:00
B1F., No.2, Ln. 26, Sec. 2, Zhongshan N. Rd., Zhongshan Dist., Taipei City
www.ppaper.net   www.facebook.com/PPAPERshop

Brandesign®

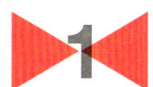

The Source of Positivity
p.10-55

Brands Love Kawaii
p.56-103

Creative Source from Food
p.104-151

The Source of Positivity

BIOVIDEO

Design: Anagrama ˙ 2013
Photography: Caroga

Biovideo is a project built to help new parents experience and enjoy the initial moments their babies are born without worrying about capturing them. With a belief that every baby deserves his or her very own Biovideo, the company shoots films about the baby's first days at the hospital and then uploads them online so as to be viewed and shared. The brand logo is simple and clear while communicates baby vibes by using white and baby blue colour and the striking red is chosen to prevent it from falling into certain unremarkable cliche.

The Source of Positivity

BADABOOM

Design: Kind

Badaboom is an emerging textile company which attachs great importance to brand identity. Kind was asked to renew their visual identity. The main identity uses the symbol of bamboo which shows the textile material. At the same time those posters express the vitality of this brand with bright colours and lovely babies and children.

The Source of Positivity

CEE IDENTITY

*Design: Vanessa Eckstein, Miki Arai & Kevin Boothe * Blok Design * 2014*

CEE Identity is designed for Coalition for Engaged Education (L.A.), an organization aiming to support society's most vulnerable youth through education that inspires them to find and realize their own potential. The logo, both word mark and icon, serves as a new identity for the organization to signal its intent to expand its mission to a national level, reflecting CEE's transforming and uplifting process of providing support for their students. By turning CEE into a verb, CEE Identity emphasizes its own beliefs of helping its students gain strength, joy and dignity.

The Source of Positivity

CRAIG & KARL FOR KIEHL'S

Design: Craig & Karl ° 2014

While working on the project Craig & Karl for Kiehl's, the two artists Craig and Karl started by creating a New York scene for the shop windows and then created a variety of faces representing characters that might be encountered on 3rd Avenue near the Kiehl's flagship. All sorts of New York iconography are infused amongst the faces such as a Statue of Liberty reference, a hot dog etc. In terms of the product labels, a more festive approach is adopted to celebrate the season of release. Loose references such as images of donuts and bagels are also tucked inside the artwork to the holiday season.

The Source of Positivity

FIVE / 五

Design: Koh Min Yu ° 2013

By condensing the 10 different types of divinations into graphical form, Koh Min Yu creates a highly handcrafted divination-themed collector's edition box set--FIVE/五 for her project's mock client, Phaidon Press. Holding the publications in hand, readers can feel the material carefully selected and every thread binded into it. From Koh Min Yu's perspective, FIVE/五 enables readers to have an interactive experience through the 10 different types of divination due to this ancient art's being used to foretell future and enhance one's understanding about himself/herself.

The Source of Positivity

NOA RELAXATION

Design: Yashar Niknam & Carl Du Rietz ° Super Tuesday & No Picnic ° 2014
Photography: Tomas Monka

Design agency Super Tuesday was invited to be involved in the project Noa Relaxation, also known as a new drink brand with natural ingredients that helps to reduce stress as well as increase mental capacity. The agency was responsible for brand identity and packaging design. The structural /shape design of the bottle was carried in collaboration with the agency No Picnic. Noa Relaxation was launched in August in Stockholm, Sweden with flavours Elderflower/Rhubarb, Crabapple/Gooseberry and Blueberry/Birch Sap!

SIX & FIVE BRANDING IDENTITY

Design: Andy Reisinger & Ezequiel Pini, Six & Five Studio® 2014

Six & Five Branding Identity is a piece of work from studio Six & Five, a contemporary art studio based in Buenos Aires exploring the frontier zone between art and design. The two founders, Andy Reisinger and Ezequiel Pini, are both Art Directors and Graphic Designers. With their vivid imagination, poetic compositions, sharp minds and slick skills, Six & Five becomes a hit in the uniqueness and purity of its results. "We always try to find an alternative way to see things, so this project represents how we imagined and developed our brand identity."

REDBERRY

Design: Anagrama ° 2013
Photography: Caroga

Redberry is a shoe store adopting the typical American footwear retailer / outlet store vibe and aiming to introduce the American concept of providing branded footwear at affordable prices for the general public.

Based on its name, the iconic logo is designed by simplifying a raspberry's unique shape and the typographic style and the main single-colour selection within the identity so as to create an industrial / modern style. As to the interior design, industrial materials such as metal and concrete are used to immerse the consumers in a factory-like setting and meanwhile the use of raw finishes, such as the gridded metal shelves, increases the brand's industrial feel and rounds it up perfectly.

The Source of Positivity

HORNHUSET

Design: Tobias Ottomar & Thomas Andersson ° Planet Creative ° 2013
Photography: Simon Bajada

Hornhuset is a bustling little square somewhere around Stockholm, Sweden. Trying to convey a Mediterranean atmosphere, studio Planet Creative chooses fresh bold colours such as ocean blue, bright yellow and ivory white that offers a sunshine beach feeling of summer.

The Source of Positivity

SHORT WAVES FESTIVAL 2014

Design: Michał Mierzwa & Mateusz Witkowski & Tomasz Biskup ° Uniforma ° 2014
Photography: Tomasz Biskup

Tomasz Biskup and Studio Uniforma together created the visual identity for the six edition of the most important short film festival in Poland - Short Waves Festival 2014. Aiming to convey a sense of playfulness, creativity, fresh and youthful quality of this cultural event, they tried to make the best of simple objects of everyday use with attention to the colour and shape and set designs through taking photographs of them without any special effects or collages.

The Source of Positivity

SID LEE LAND

Design: Marie-Elaine Benoit, Nadine Brunet, Alice Ware, Émilie Salles · Thomas Pison · 2014

Different from traditional internships, Sid Lee Land aims to offer the coolest and most rewarding experience to those young while aspiring interns, far from the position of "fax assistant". Instead of those dreadful employment forms and uninspiring booths at the entrance of universities, Sid Lee opted for a multiplatform, playful, and colourful campaign by using visual language, experiential site, animated clips, posters, humorous writing, and "intern kit".

GORKY PARK ICECREAM

Design: Anastasia Genkina ˚ 2014
Photography: Grigory Sobchenko & Anastasia Genkina

Gorky Park Icecream has been a treat inseparable from a walk in the Moscow Gorky Park for decades. Its classical flavour of creamy vanilla and waffle cone has become a memory of childhood for several generations. The packaging design of it was presented by the designer Anastasia Genkina. With an aim to connect the historical value with modern taste, the designer tried to develop patterns from the key symbols of the Park life. Each flavour has its own pattern which is fresh as well as elegant.

BALLOON
GREETING CARDS

Design: Unelefante ˚ 2012-2014
Photography: Caroga

Being the founder of the studio UNELEFANTE, Tatiana Sánchez views the studio's mission as transforming the ordinary into extraordinary experiences by treasuring creativity, detail and craftsmanship. Inspired by the film "The Red Balloon" and certain kind of nostalgia, UNELEFANTE created the gigantic helium balloons decorated with handmade paper tassels, based on which comes the Balloon greeting cards. It is one of the magical gift collections that include gigantic balloons, piñatas, artisan chocolates and other unique products. The balloons can be custom made with messages printed on them and the person who receives the special greeting card will have to inflate the balloon to discover the message on it, offering pleasure of giving and surprising.

DIALOGUE WITH

Kit Cheuk
p43-p45

Fredrik Öst
p46-p51

Ana Milena Hernández Palacios
p52-p55

DIALOGUE WITH
Kit Cheuk

Can you share your childhood dream?
I just simply loved drawing when I was a child and tried to be a painter or artist before but finally went into the design industry.

How did you become a brand designer?
Basically it all started with my interest in design; brand design is fundamental to the brand itself which includes marketing and positioning. Brand design needs rational and logical thinking compared with other graphic designing. And with this ideal in mind, I finally chose to be a brand designer.

Can you share the changes of brand designs in the last few years?
The sense of aesthetic and taste have been the essential elements for the last few years, and concept is important too but it seems that it's not the priority for brand exercise nowadays.

As a brand designer, how do you convey positivity and maintain constant creativity?
Honestly from my past experience, it can be hard and depressing at times as a designer. However, it is a duty to provide the best design solution to the client and as a good designer, one should always strive to propose and contribute something innovative and captivating to the industry.

Certain design elements build an image full of positivity. Which design elements are they?
Most designers and clients think brand design is merely a logo or a name card. But I think the most critical element for brand design is to build up a core value and inject a spirit by visual elements, allowing the brand to develop its culture and style and not just rely on the appearance of the design.

What kind of brand design can excite you?
All brand designs can be good references, not only the successful cases but also the unsuccessful ones. We sometimes spend a lot of time to catch up to the design trend but I find interest in studying the design approach in line with trend in order to analyse the needs of the market. ®

media tube

MEDIA TUBE

*Design: Not Available (NA) * 2014*

Being an independent art gallery in Shanghai, China that exhibits contemporary media arts within a progressive curatorial framework, Media Tube is also the project by studio Not Available (NA). The design of its visual identity is built in the art of broadcast in contemporary style with an official tailored typeface for its publication use.

DIALOGUE WITH

Fredrik Öst
Founder & Creative Director of SNASK

Can you share your childhood dream?

My childhood dream was to become successful enough to be on television. I used to watch a lot of MTV and other shows and pictured myself on the television. It was hard but with enough fantasy and focus I sometimes managed to see myself there. I was always told by my mother "You can do anything as long as you want to".

How did you become a brand designer?

I got interested when two students from a graphic design programme talked to us when I was 15. But it wasn't until I was studying psychology and started producing flyers, for a club night some friends and me arranged, that I got into branding and design.

Can you share the changes of brand designs in the last few years?

Online is the right word. People are extremely aware of what's happening on a global scale. Suddenly you could become famous globally by simply being good at what you're doing instead of having the right contacts. I mean forums such as Behance, Pinterest, Vimeo, etc.

As a brand designer, how do you convey positivity and maintain constant creativity?

We're all for making enemies and gaining fans. I don't believe in brands that are neutral. They should have opinions to stand up for and be very obvious in their communication. When it comes to creativity, to assimilate good culture and you would become creative. Books, music that you choose (not that you get fed) and great dinners, etc., these could all be sources of inspiration.

Certain design elements build an image full of positivity. Which design elements are they?

I am not sure about it. You can't say that a colour is more positive than another, it's all about every person's own taste and view as well as the context it's placed in.

What kind of brand design can excite you?

I would prefer brands that stand out and stand up for something. For example, when brands stand up for feminism I think they're on the right track. Brands that stay neutral and don't state their own positions are many years behind. Read this in 20 years and you'll see why. ®

MALMÖ FESTIVAL 2014

Design: Jens Nilsson ° SNASK ° 2014
Photography: Nils Bergendahl & Anders Sipinen

Malmö Festival 2014, Scandinavia's largest city festival, is also a graphic design work from Studio SNASK. SNASK creates a physical art installation measuring 13×8 meters which is probably the world's largest art installation, enabling people to climb or jump on it. It takes 900 hours with 14 people to finish the work. 10,000 nails, 175 litres of paint, 280 plywood sheets are used to produce the identity and a skylift is rented to photograph it 30 meters up in the air.

The Source of Positivity

Logotype / Flexible logotype for collaborators

Display Typography – Example

Colors

Typography – Display

Typography – Body

ABCDEFGHIJKLMOPQRSTUVWXYZÅÄÖ
abcdefghijklmo
pqrstuvwxyzåäö
0123456789!?.:

DANCE ♥ STOCKHOLM

*Design: Magdalena Czarnecki * SNASK * 2014*

Dance ♥ Stockholm is a five-day international contemporary dance festival. Studio SNASK is invited to help design the festival in a brand new way. Through using a colourful approach, SNASK tries to make contemporary dance fun and open instead of serious and behind closed doors. The project covers graphic identity, graphic guidelines, catalogue design, how to communicate, and production of various branded material: ads, posters, festive balloons and so on.

DIALOGUE WITH
Ana Milena Hernández Palacios

Masquespacio Studio

Can you share your childhood dream?
As a child I've been introduced to the world of decoration by my mother, who was an event planner. I've always been interested by crafts just like my mother. Maybe I can see my actual career, is like a childhood dream coming true.

How did you become a brand designer?
I've always being interested in brands and in particular the brand experience. When I founded Masquespacio 4 years ago with my partner specializing in marketing, I had the chance to learn more about branding and brand culture.

Can you share the changes of brand designs in the last few years?
More and more designers and architects from different disciplines are incorporating branding into their services. We think it's a positive evolution on one hand as we think that brand and space are inseparable. Brand space is not just about adding a logo to a space, for us it is the trick to translate the brands value through its selling point.

As a brand designer, how do you convey positivity and maintain constant creativity?
We think every brand has something positive to transmit: its history, its culture or maybe just the people behind it. We think that transmitting positivity is just a matter of being able to work for a brand that transmits positivity through one of the factors before mentioned, but mainly if there is positive relation between our client and us, it's pretty easy to create it for the brand.

Certain design elements build an image full of positivity. Which design elements are they?
We think colours are a very good element to create emotions, but also textures and materials. We like to use them all, blend them or just separately.

What kind of brand design can excite you?
We are particularly in love with Aesop. We think their selling points are a perfect example of how to support a strong brand with a strong image through its selling point. Every Aesop store is different, perfectly adapting to local culture, but still recognizable. An Aesop store doesn't need an Aesop logo to be recognizable. ®

DOCTOR MANZANA

Design: Ana Milena Hernández Palacios "Masquespacio" 2013
Photography: David Rodríguez

Masquespacio designed the brand and space for Doctor Manzana, an online store specialized in providing technical service for smartphones and tablets and selling design gadgets for mobile devices. The design consists of the re-branding of Doctor Manzana and the space of its first physical point of sale located in Valencia, Spain. Inspired by the principal axe of the company'the touchscreen', the logotype starts from a reflection of it that creates an angle of 54 degrees appearing continually in their original form or defragmented into different applications to the graphic and interior design. In terms of the colours, blue and green are used as a reference to the first word of the brand - doctor. In order not to create a conventional design, the salmon colour for the fashionists and the purple for the freaks.

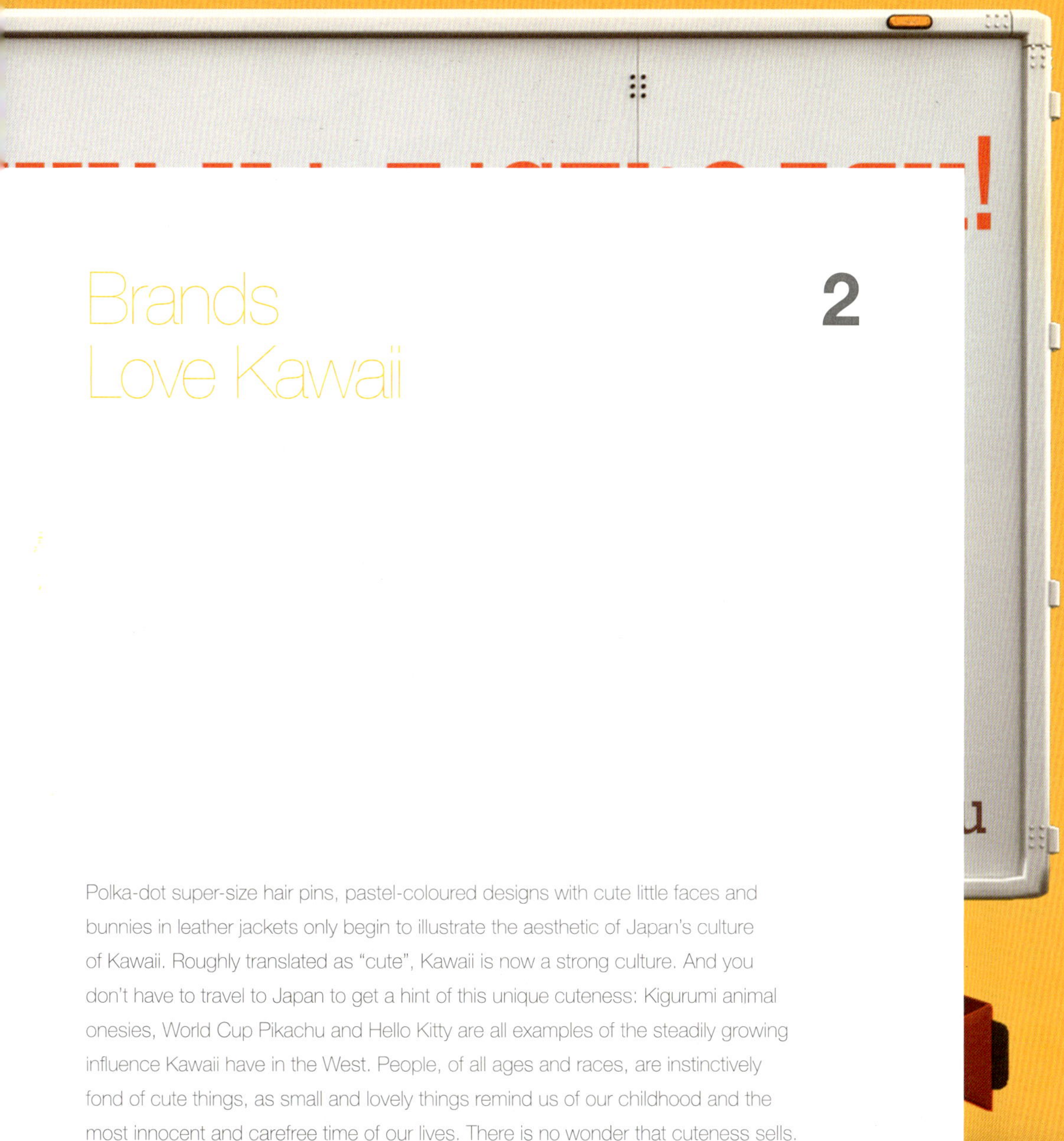

Brands Love Kawaii

2

Polka-dot super-size hair pins, pastel-coloured designs with cute little faces and bunnies in leather jackets only begin to illustrate the aesthetic of Japan's culture of Kawaii. Roughly translated as "cute", Kawaii is now a strong culture. And you don't have to travel to Japan to get a hint of this unique cuteness: Kigurumi animal onesies, World Cup Pikachu and Hello Kitty are all examples of the steadily growing influence Kawaii have in the West. People, of all ages and races, are instinctively fond of cute things, as small and lovely things remind us of our childhood and the most innocent and carefree time of our lives. There is no wonder that cuteness sells.

The culture of Kawaii has spread all over the world as a universal trend with arrays of inspirations and inventions. Besides the obviously cute product--toys, we often see packaging designs and branding designs of other products with cute illustrations and characters. Candies, for example, being kids' favourite, when dressed with cute packaging "outfit", tend to attract not only kids but also adults. The childish yet fun design prompts an image of playfulness and it suits the marketing of candies, bringing customers the experience of being kids again.

KUKLACHEV'S CATS THEATRE

Design: Tanya Mikolaevskaya ° 2014

Moscow Cats Theatre is the only theatre in the world where cats are the main actors. It was created by Yuri Kuklachev in the 90's and since then has been a favourite place for children. The theatre needed a more modern and recognisable style, and needed to show the cats apartments and pet the fluffy actors while children visiting the theatre. Graphics are inspired by traditional Russian illustration style of Lubok, characterized by simple and funny graphics.

театр кошек
КУКЛАЧЕВА

сцена гардероб буфет билеты

музей ж м

The Calendar Who Knew Too Much

*Design: VASAVA * 2014*

This project contains two collections of agenda, pad and calendars containing 365 trifles or curiosities. Designers have compiled and illustrated them so that they may accompany the owners during 2015. Now kicking off a new year with white canvas in front of you, on which to express your hopes and dreams.

Brands Love Kawaii

SHIROKUMA
NO OKOME

Design: Ryuta Ishikawa ° Frame inc. ° 2013

The logo is a polar bear with the shape of rice as his nose. Polar bear gives people a sense of warmness. The shape of rice as the contouring represents that the process of producing rice takes a lot of time and efforts.

BROSMIND DECK

Design: Juan & Alejandro Mingarro " Brosmind " 2014
Photography: Carles Pradas

BROSMIND DECK is the first playing card set fully designed by the brothers for the acclaimed card company Bicycle. Brosmind is well known for their characters, every card has a unique character that goes from food, robots, abstract and pots depending on the suits. And even the back of the cards has a beautiful design where customers can easily recognise the optimistic Brosmind's style.

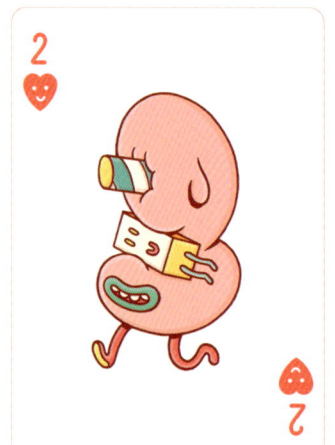

Brands Love Kawaii

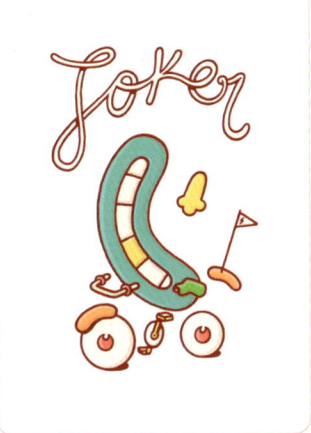

KOKESHI MATCHES

Design: Kumi Hirasaka ˚ Kokeshi Match Factory
Photography: Shinsuke Nishiumi

In 1994 designer Kumi made a matchbox for a group exhibition. She drew face of KOKESHI, a traditional Japanese wooden doll by hand on each match. Inspired by this she created a series of matchbox with various characters.

MONSTER CANDY

Design: Charlotte Olsen ˚ 2014

Using a strong colour palette and sticking to a strong line, Charlotte Olsen focused on making MONSTER CANDY, a series of candy boxes, look as fun and playful as possible.
To catch people's attention and give them a good laugh, these little candy monster gift boxes look like they've literally eaten themselves to death with candy bursting through.

Brands Love Kawaii

CADBURY'S DAIRY MILK BUTTONS

Design: Natalie Chung ° Pearlfisher

Pearlfisher redesigned the packaging for Cadbury's Dairy Milk Buttons and Giant Buttons.

The new design uses 5 different graphic expressions for the milk chocolate variant. These are familiar animals (a monkey, cat, pig, owl and panda) plus one additional animal to distinguish the white chocolate variant (a penguin). The design execution uses the image of the product for the "button" eyes of each animal. The bright, engaging colours work over both Cadbury Dairy Milk Buttons and Giant Buttons to enhance the playful spirit of the brand. The iconic Cadbury colour is not only obvious but also not obtrusive within the 9 palette gravure on metallic substrate, matt laminated to achieve the lustrous purple.

SUPER FRUITS DOJO

Design: Carlos Higuera ° 2014

The initial idea of the game Super Fruits Dojo was that fruits help kids to fight the junk food. The original logo of the game is in Japanese. Carlos believes that Japanese typographies give these illustrations a Kawaii look. He also created all those Characters with the same cute and childish style.

WU KE XING

Design: SUSU & YAO ° 1983 ASIA

Wu Ke Xing is a premium art formative education/publishing house. Differentiate from the force-feed style art training centers on market today, Wu Ke Xing exhales their creativity thinking based on kids' real need. The design inspiration for this program is that "studying is as fun as making friends". Five lovely kids who play different personalities will feed into the five-pointed star as the brand element. In order to set up the whole branding experience to the audience, this visual concept is applied in stationary, daily-use, fashion wearing and space.

ZOMBIS

Design: Snorri Snorrason, Thorvaldur Gunnarsson, Bragi Skulason,
Gudlaugur Adalsteinsson & Hrafn Gunnarsson ° Brandenburg ° 2014

Zombis is a new brand of freezer pops that are created to be eaten out of the top of a zombie's head. The design and packaging was done by Brandenburg, who recruited 24 zombies from all over Iceland to take part in this project. Each one has a name, a brief death-ography and a surprisingly tasty and colourful brain – strawberry, raspberry or pistachio flavored.

UOVO KIDS

Design: Sara Bianchi & Andrea Zambardi " Atto" 2014
Photography: Andrea Zambardi & Lorenza Daverio

Uovo Kids is the most important Italian festival dedicated to contemporary creativity for kids (0-12). Sara Bianchi and Andrea Zambardi, from Atto were commissioned to create identity for this festival. They imagined surreal stories involving flying bears, spatial dogs, and naughty aliens for the concept and developed posters, programs, gadgets, promotional video, and signage for the whole festival.

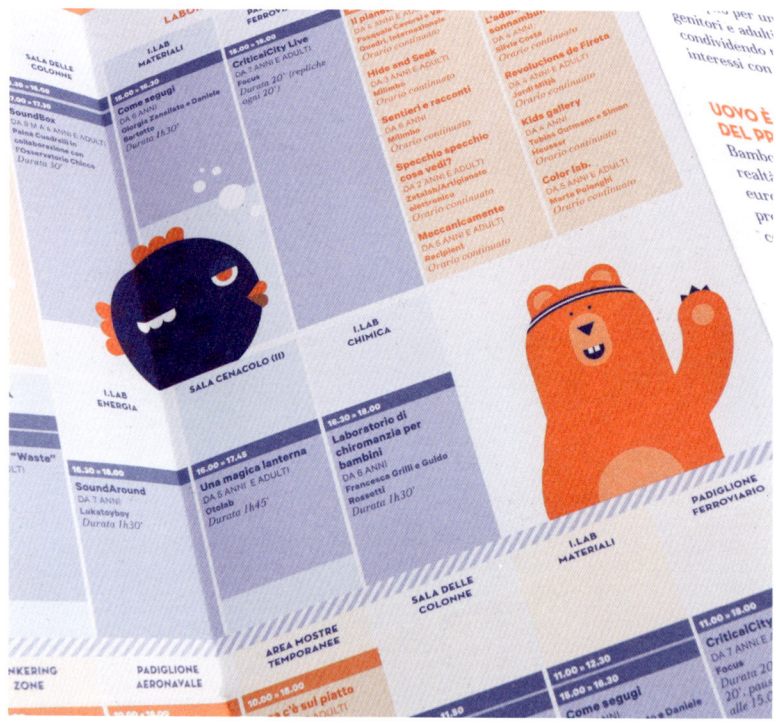

DILLII

Design: Rúben Rodrigues ¨ 2014

Dillii with the motto "Dillicious & Dillirious" is a project of the packaging and branding identity for the organic cookies brand. As the brief was not that restrictive, designer Rúben Rodrigues tried to have the most fun with it. He made it very visual but at the same time with the concern in conciliating the interact part with the illustrations, showing new narratives and the sensations in tasting the cookies (ice cream man melting for hot spicy cookies, and astronaut flying to the outer space for the mint cookies) making it fun to interact, just like opening a wrapped gift releasing all the surprise and joy in somebody's smile.

LE CHOCOLAT DES FRANÇAIS

Design: Paul-Henri Masson ° Le chocolat des Francais ° 2014

This is the visual identity of Le chocolat des Français. This chocolate has an original feature: beyond its great taste qualities, it is 100% made in France. This is obviously an exciting area to exploit. Designer Paul-Henri Masson thought of calling it Le chocolat des Français in order to outstand from Belgian and Swiss chocolate. The designer then contacted fifty french illustrators with only one restraint: evoking France. The result is a cheerful and colourful melting pot, a profusion of disparate pictures which nevertheless work very well together.

MICHELLE'S BAKERY

*Design: Anya Aleksandrova * G-sign Agency*

Bright and cheerful branding for French bakery in Moscow, the project is done in collaboration with G-sign Agency. With the aim to convey the joyful atmosphere and a bit of Paris madness, Anya Aleksandrova and G-sign Agency did not want to use the standard approach, as Provence or retro, they want fun! Children who come to the bakery would love the design - bright colours and cute bulldog. They can also buy cakes and pack them in the original box, which is nice to bring home or give to someone.

PACKING FOR THE OATMEAL COOKIES IN CHOCOLATE

Design: An Palahniuk & Alexander Petrov ˚ TWET art group ˚ 2014

TWET art-group developed cute characters – hares consuming the product, and a unique grapheme "Get Ready for a Daily Dozen !" It was important to show both the oatmeal cookies and the chocolate in the image of the product. Special attention was paid to work with texts on the packing to make it as informative as possible and appealing.

LIMITED EDITION HANDMADE EGGROLL PACKAGING FOR LUNG CHING FOOD

Design: Victor Branding Design Corp ˙ 2014

Based on a playful game, this limited edition eggroll packaging design has a unique structure. Inspired by circus elements, illustrator BaNAna created two cute little characters - Mr. Peanut and Ms. Almond - with bold colours. Two main colours blue and yellow were applied to differentiate flavours. Its beautiful graphic design and unique handle make it the perfect gift to carry home.

FARINHA LÁCTEA NESTLÉ

Design: Mariana Ikuta & Isabela Rodrigues ° Isabela Rodrigues
Sweety Branding Studio ° 2014

Invited by Nestlé to design for the a collectible packaging of Farinha Láctea brand, Mariana and Isabela tried to design in a way that enables the packaging to be reused in a creative and decorative way, serving as an emotional bond between the brand and the consumers.

Lovely exquisite Icons and candy colours are infused into the design so as to convey a sense of family coziness, warmth as well as modernity while the gold paint highlights the premium aspect.

SIDE DISH CUP

Design: Maiko Matsue & Shunsuke Satake ° G_graphics Inc ° 2014
Photography: Kodai Nakamura

Studio Maruki promoted a new two-commodity (body cup & package) side dish cup which is called "Thank you side dish cup of the world". Each piece was designed with the words "Thank you" in different languages and have a specific illustration responding the language. This beautiful design brings customers a sense of elegance and friendliness.

DIALOGUE WITH
Manami Okazaki

Manami Okazaki is an author of numerous Japanese culture books. Her best selling titles are Kokeshi, from Tohoku with Love, Kawaii, Japan's Culture of Cute and Kicks Japan. She is a contributor for many magazines internationally and blogs for the Wall Street Journal. She is now making a series on toy camera photography.

Some argues that Kawaii can not be translated into any specific English word, only similar to "cute" or "lovely". What is the definition of Kawaii in your eyes?

Kawaii roughly translates to 'cute', and describes the adorable physical features that kids and baby animals have, and anything that breeds feelings of love and the maternal instinct to care and protect. The word 'Kawaii' can be used to describe the atmosphere or perceived qualities of something, as well as its appearance. Nowadays, 'Kawaii' is a complimentary adjective applied in mind-bogglingly varied ways: it is synonymous with beautiful, lovable, addictive, cool, funny, even ugly but endearing, quirky and gross. It is hard to define, because in Japan, the meaning has evolved so many times. In this way, the notoriously fickle consumer demographic in Japan doesn't get sick of Kawaii, as it is used in so many different directions, often iconically..

How do these identifying and unique elements of Kawaii styles, such as the romantic pastel colours and cartoon characters of all sorts, contribute to the design industries?

I think it is more that the design industries are utilizing the Kawaii aesthetic as a way to appeal to consumers who are obsessed with cute products. I think the main reason Kawaii has become such a movement in Japan is because it is so versatile.

The top luminaries and creators in the fields of fashion, character design, food design, and even interior, architecture, and robotics use Kawaii sensibilities in their work.

Is Kawaii a good marketing strategy? How do brands benefit from adopting the Kawaii styles?

In the Japanese market, by making something Kawaii, it becomes accessible, interesting and funny. At its heart, it is similar to traditional gift wrapping – it is taking the extra step to make something aesthetically pleasing and charming. When I interviewed the designer of Paro, the robotic seal in Japan, he also mentioned that his patients (the elderly and people in disaster trauma, etc) find this cute robot healing, and comforting.

On the flipside, there is this notion that to make something Kawaii in Japan, it will become accepted and liked -- so there are some truly hilarious and insidious uses of Kawaii design (the Tokyo metropolitan police force, Hamaoka nuclear power plant, even a jail in Northern Japan all have Kawaii mascots).

In overseas, I think Kawaii culture is seen as something fresh and exotic, so it has an element of being an alternative to the mainstream. A lot of people are appreciating Kawaii culture in places like the US and France because they grew up with Manga, so theyalso find it nostalgic. Additionally, celebrities and fashion designers find inspiration from Japanese youth styles and popular culture.

While I think a lot of it is due to globalization, and people being interested in cultures other than one's own, I was told by Sanrio Europe that a lot of people don't even know that Hello Kitty is from Japan, and it is the universal and simple design that makes her such a hit. In the case of Hello Kitty, there is a slight sense of humour and irony as well that completely incongruous brands like Stussy, Swarovski and the rock band KISS are teaming up with Hello Kitty—but somehow it works, and in doing so, they are also widening their audience.

Does Kawaii culture have a growing influence outside of Japan now? How so?

People globally have been embracing elements of Kawaii culture in many ways - although I have to say, it is still seen as a new, exotic trend, and is not on the level of ubiquity as in Japan. I will not suggest that it will become the dominant pop cultural aesthetic abroad, as it is in Japan, but there are signs that it is a viable alternative to youth who don't feel an affinity to mainstream options, for example, American teens who can't relate to overly sexual pop music stars and so on.

There are also shops catering to Kawaii culture lovers globally such as ShopKawaii, Tofucute, Kawaii-land (the list is long) and too many Kawaii culture themed websites to mention. France is the second biggest consumer of manga globally, and their knowledge of Japanese culture in general is very rich. I was really surprised at how many people were into Kawaii fashion in Paris when I went to the Japan Expo this year, which attracted over 200,000 people.

How is Japanese Kawaii culture different from the one in rest of the world?

Overall, it is the same concept. People associate the word Kawaii with things or people that are cute, innocent, sweet, need to be nurtured, protected and loved. Kawaii things and people embody childlike qualities and breed feelings of joy. Overseas, people equate Kawaii with Japanese culture, whereas, in Japan, Kawaii culture is historically quite often an amalgamation of East and West. Early pioneers of the Kawaii aesthetic such as illustrators Macoto Takahashi and Eico Hanamura were incorporating western fashion or motifs into their work, and were heavily influenced by the things they saw in the post war occupation.

Likewise, the mecca for Kawaii youth fashion, the Harajuku neighborhood in West Tokyo housed American GI's during the American occupation post war. Many of the first shops in Harajuku catered to Americans, and Japanese youth would go there to see an exotic, foreign culture. As such, it came to represent a place where new, innovative ideas and things could proliferate, and many foreign subcultures (albeit with a Japanese twist) burgeoned in the area.

I should also add that in the US (not so much Europe) Kawaii culture is sometimes seen as a pan-Asian culture, not just solely Japanese. Additionally, many of the people who embrace Kawaii art, craft, fashion and make-up are Vietnamese American, Chinese American and so on.

KAWAII FASHION USUALLY EMBODIES A PLAYFUL, COLOURFUL, CHILDLIKE, AND INNOCENT ATMOSPHERE.

In your opinion, have other countries created their own sub cultures based on Kawaii style?

Kawaii fashion usually embodies a playful, colourful, childlike, and innocent atmosphere. A lot of Kawaii fashion is influenced by early fashion illustrators and manga artists, and they have an almost cartoon-like aesthetic. Overseas, it is not so much that new subcultures are developing; they are co-opting Japanese subcultures but are interpreting them in different ways. For example, Kawaii fashion in America is more "cool" and aligned with subcultures like punk and there are even huge graffiti exhibitions with a Hello Kitty theme. I think generally, in the west, subculture people tend to be quite gregarious, and flamboyant, and the clothing is an extension of their outgoing personalities. However, I have met many people who get into Kawaii fashion essentially for the same reasons. Some also see Kawaii fashion as a way to celebrate femininity.

Creative Source from Food

3

Surrounded by handsome chick celebrities, graceful cows and beautiful butterflies, you might think you are in a zoo, but it turns out that you are standing in the centre of a grocery or a supermarket in a crowded city. When those fresh vegetables, fruits and meat wear a new clothing, they immediately acquire new identities and convey a colourful brand culture. A small package might tell you a story of an organic farm, depict the happy life of all animals, or even inform you a whole new life style. When we enter into those groceries and markets, what exactly are we buying? Simply prepare some food for next meal? Or an organic idea, a healthy lifestyle or even the love for your homeland?

We start this journey to food, hope those delicious foods not only provides you nutrition and energy, but also becomes a source for creative thinking.

CORELLA

Design: Marc Navarro, Albert Martinez ° Fauna ° 2014
Photography: Xavier González

The project was to create the branding and packaging for Corella, a butcher shop in Sant Cugat. The main objective was to show the clients which part they are going to buy. Taking the interior design into account, designers decided to use the red frames as a corporate element for the brand, symbolizing the transparency of the meat working process. The red frame also shows the specific piece of meat that clients are going to buy.

For the premium packs, designers replaced the red colour for a gold stamping emphasizing the exclusivity and quality. Once the label structure was firmly in place, they developed the "special nens" (for kids) labels, replacing the animal illustrations for origami animals.

JUST LAID

Design: Springetts Brand Design Consultants ° 2013

As part of an ongoing work with Noble Foods, the designers were asked to develop concepts that explored how eggs could better satisfy or respond to consumer needs. Their solution was to emphasise the benefit of locally laid eggs to consumers through a cheeky brand name that reinforces the idea of freshly laid eggs straight from the hen. The creative execution is a selection of playful, caricatures of hens laying eggs with three different poses/expressions for each of the three variants.

BUTTERFLY KINGDOM TAIWAN TEA

Design: Xie Yauzer ˚ TROONIONDesign ˚ 2014

One of the beautiful insects that the designer was enchanted by is butterflies. The song, Butterfly Flies, which was heard and sung in his childhood reminds him once more of the carefree lives. Inspired by those butterflies, the designer chooses to express this unique Butterfly Kingdom Taiwan Tea with beautiful butterflies on the package.

1 Week Salad

Design: Oki Sato ° Nendo ° 2014
Photography: Akihiro Yoshida

1 Week Salad project has turned a former semi-conductor factory into a farm, reuses a sealed, bacteria-excluding room to grow organic vegetables. The salad enjoys the great advantage of lasting in the refrigerator for nearly a week, since it has no contact with insects or bacteria. To emphasise its natural freshness, designer selected beverage containers and designed internal paper packaging. Each of the 31 days uses different colours and typefaces for the stand-up numbers so that the products' shelf experience is fresh and constantly changing. Ultimately, they wanted to design a product that would target two characteristics not usually experienced in shops: long-life preservation and how safe supplies contribute to daily life.

Creative Source from Food

ANGUS 6

Design: Jeyoun Lee, Hanme Chol, Bobae Kim & Youngji Jung " Eggplant Factory " 2014
Photography: Jaeseung Shim & Seunghui Lee

Angus 6 is a premium beef brand that sells only Australian beef. The concept behind this brand is "The Great Inheritance". To emphasise the great nature of Australia, designers wanted to give an exquisite high quality brand look by using the strong black and white colour palette and spare of beefy red. The traditional serif typeface (both English and Korean) adds authentic look to the brand as well.

Creative Source from Food

BLUE GOOSE

Design: Dave Roberts, Tom Koukodimos, Flavio Carvalho, Anna Sera Garcia, Oleg Portnoy, Emily Patterson, Pip Scowcroft, Laurent Abesdris & Ben Kwok ° Sid Lee ° 2014
Photography: Rob Fiocca & Steve Krug

Sid Lee developed the brand identity and packaging design for an organic food brand Blue Goose, working with illustrator Ben Kwok to develop the cow, chicken and fish illustrations that serve as the focal point of the packaging. The design inside each illustration provides a rich and detailed representation of each animal's natural environment, and the conditions it was raised in. The soft, stylized approach conveyed the care that Blue Goose provides when rearing its animals and brought the brand values to life in a unique manner. The choice of using blue separated the brand from competing marques as it is a colour not traditionally associated with food.

HEADLINE

**BRANDON
BOLD ALL CAPS
THE QUICK BROWN
FOX JUMPS OVER
THE LAZY DOG**

BRANDON
BOLD ALL CAPS
THE QUICK BROWN
FOX JUMPS OVER
THE LAZY DOG

SUBHEAD

**Caecilia 85 Heavy
The quick brown
fox jumps over
the lazy dog**

Caecilia 75 Bold
The quick brown
fox jumps over
the lazy dog

THE ONLY ADDITIVE WE USE ─ IS ─ LOVE.

FISH & RICE

Design: Hailong Xiang ° 2013

Recycling and culture are keywords of this rice packaging design for Fengfan Farm Products. The one-piece design is not only structurally smart to emphasise the shape of the character, but also easy to carry. Traditional white canvas material and wax printing process enhance the theme of culture. Detailed graphic of rice and wheat presents the quality of this product.

Creative Source from Food

GIMSEL

Design: Studio Beige ° 2013
Photography: Jan Bij l & Leontien Herkelman

Studio Beige was asked to come up with an entirely new visual and brand identity for Gimsel, an organic food supermarket in Rotterdam, to appeal to a wider scope of consumers with a more pronounced profile. Studio Beige determined a communication strategy and wrote a manifest which clearly states where Gimsel stands. The logo they designed, with above the M a reference to "House Gimsel", radiates timelessness and balance.

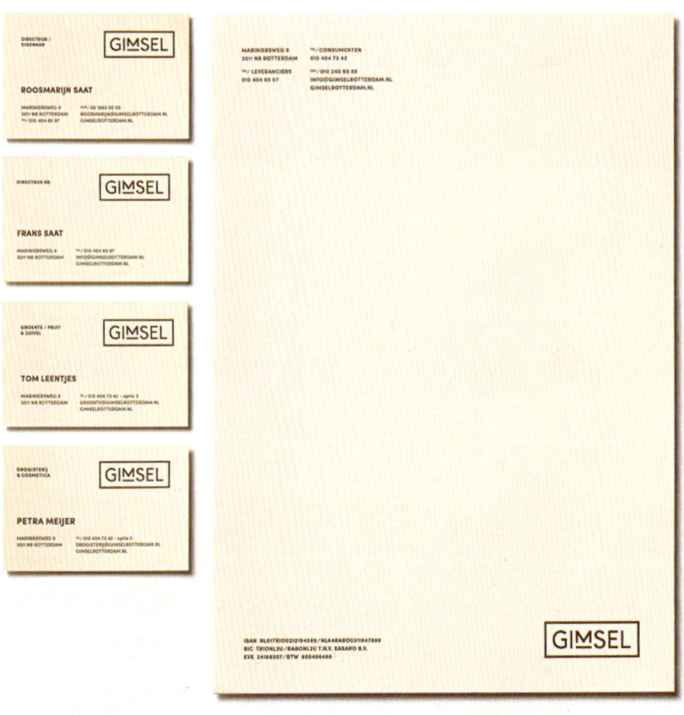

Creative Source from Food

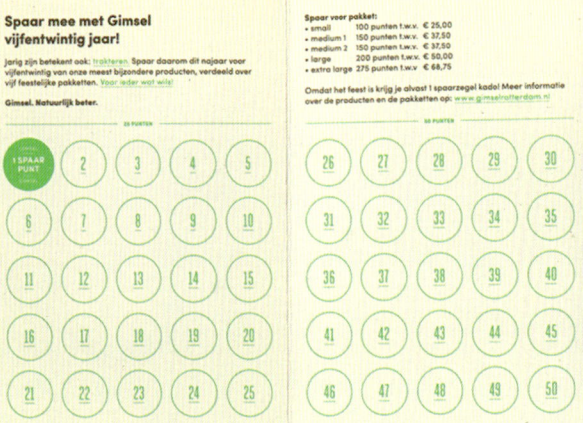

INSAL'ARTE

Design: Mirco Luzzi ° Deofficina ° 2014

Every package of fresh salad in polypropylene bag shows the initial letter of the product which is inside of it. For the realisation of every letter it has been created a sculpture made with salad's leaves which it was photographed, using the salad contained in the package. The result not only shows the fresh product contained in the package but also creates immediate recognizability when shelf stocked and the possibility to establish customer interaction having the entire alphabet at their disposal.

PAMS PRIVATE LABEL FLOUR RANGE

*Design: Paula Bunny, Angela Keoghan * Brother Design * 2013*

Designers wanted a hand-crafted feel that fitted nicely with Pams Private Label's friendly and warm personality. Their brief was to adopt a distinct personality and style to compete strongly in grocery products, and to create real stand out and appealing designs that are friendly and delightful.

QIAN'S GIFT

Design: Chong Peng ° Pesign Studio ° 2013

In response to the local's respect for nature and their Eco-friendly farming techniques, designers avoid any of industrialization in his packaging design. The paper was handmade by local people and printed with vegetable dye.

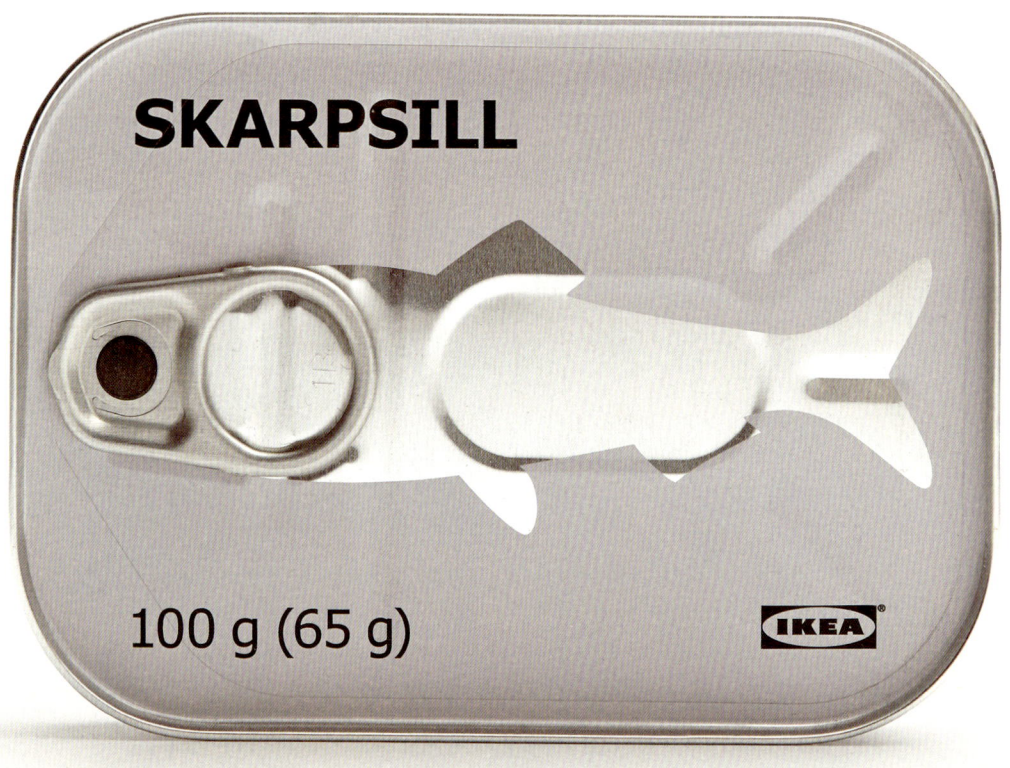

IKEA FOOD

Design: Stockholm Design Lab ° 2008-2014

IKEA wished to consolidate its café and food market operations by bringing them under IKEA Food, and introducing a wide range of own-label products. Stockholm Design Lab devised three strategies for the food packaging, based on: transparency on package, iconic illustrations and silhouettes on canned food. Removing every last scrap of unnecessary information and decoration, they were able to bring some typically IKEA-like simplicity, clarity, consistency to IKEA Food range.

SWISH®

Design: Ignacio Nicolás Vasino ˚ Empatia® ˚ 2014

From the ocean to your plate, Sweden seafood company Swish® demands perfection. In order to achieve this perfection, designer developed a deeper process of branding. With white, yellow and blue, the designer gave this newly brand a whole graphic universe.

Creative Source from Food

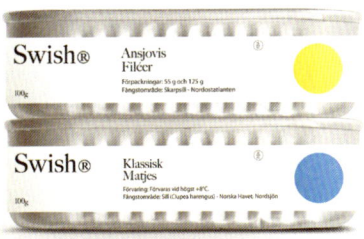

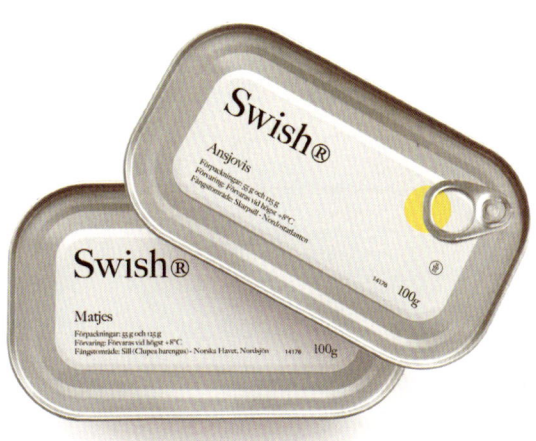

DAEBETÉ
SCENTED TEA

Design: Chung Yuan Kuo, Jui Cheng Liu, Wan Ju Lee & Jhen Ying Shih ˚ Victor Branding Design Corp. ˚ 2014

Following the delicate ancient production methods, Daebeté tea gives a special sweet fragrance which is absorbed from flowers. In addition to the traditional production process, Daebeté developed product ranges according to different flower seeds, and the right ratio of moderation leaves and flowers.

Creative Source from Food

PLUK KRUIDJE

Design: Jon Sonneveld ° Moutain Design ° 2013

The Pluk (Pick) project was commissioned by Fresh Herbs brands. By using a funny and optimistic style, character grandma becomes a contemporary icon and expresses the freshness of the product. Her dress is used as a closing sticker on the cardboard sleeve. The plastic bag is attached in the cardboard sleeve.

PLUME & Co

Design: Stephane Ricou, Marie-Pierre Fricou ° Brand Union Paris ° 2014

The concept backed by Brand Union Paris, has been offering Plume & Company, who provides organic farming for the nutrition of hens, a communication way beyond the nutritional qualities of the brand. The chickens are photographed like celebrities parading in the finest fashion shows and any lack of modesty, and they speak about the benefits of each product.

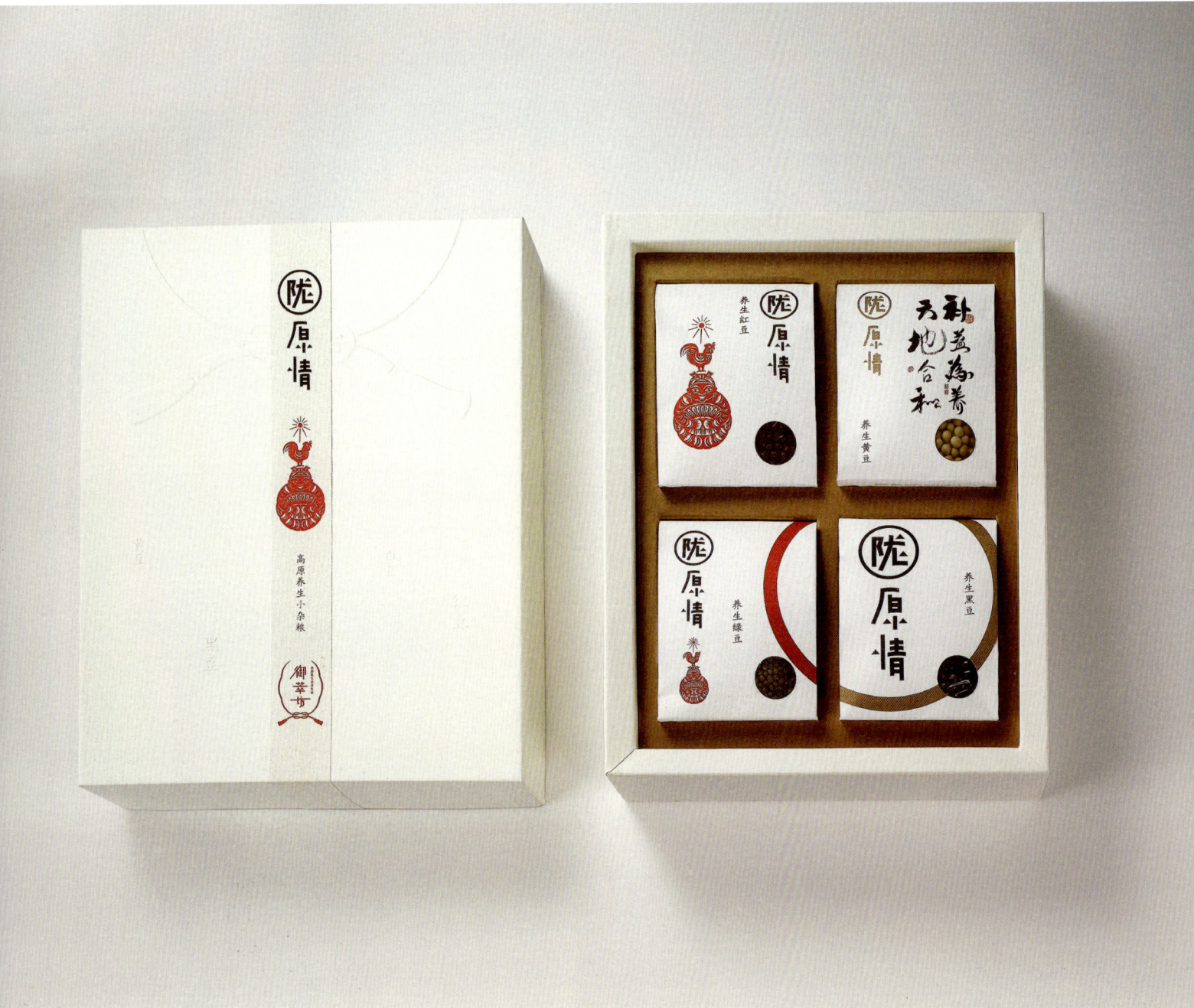

LOVE FOR LONGYUAN

Design: Shenzhen Excel Package Design, Co. Ltd

"Long" is an alternative name for Gansu Province, China. Designers created a new type for this package which represents the characteristic of this area. The main identity of this brand, in the form of paper-cut, shows the life and customs of people living in this area. The simple white surfaces are distinguished on the shelf, while the small transparent "window" allow customers a preview of those high quality beans.

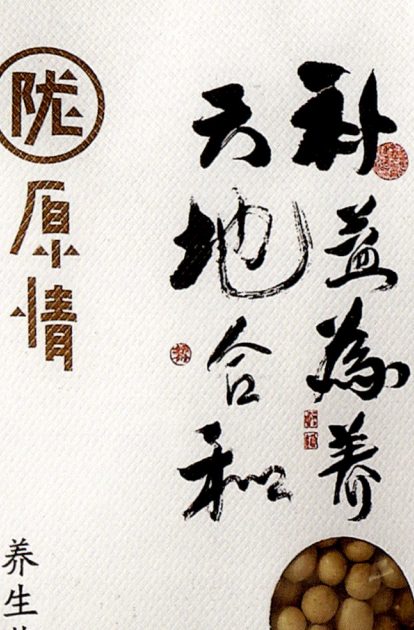

HARMONIAN

Design: Mousegraphics ° 2013

Harmonian wants a packaging design which will introduce in the most definitive way of a radical line of food products. They are actually more of 'food principles', as they all suggest a new, health-smart and taste-full way of life. Designers opted for a design which would convey the dual nature of these valuable seeds as well the harmony and balance. They came up with a strong visual statement regarding space and matter. Also the simple white surfaces - packages which are distinguished by the illusion of a cut, a twofold spindle like incision on paper.

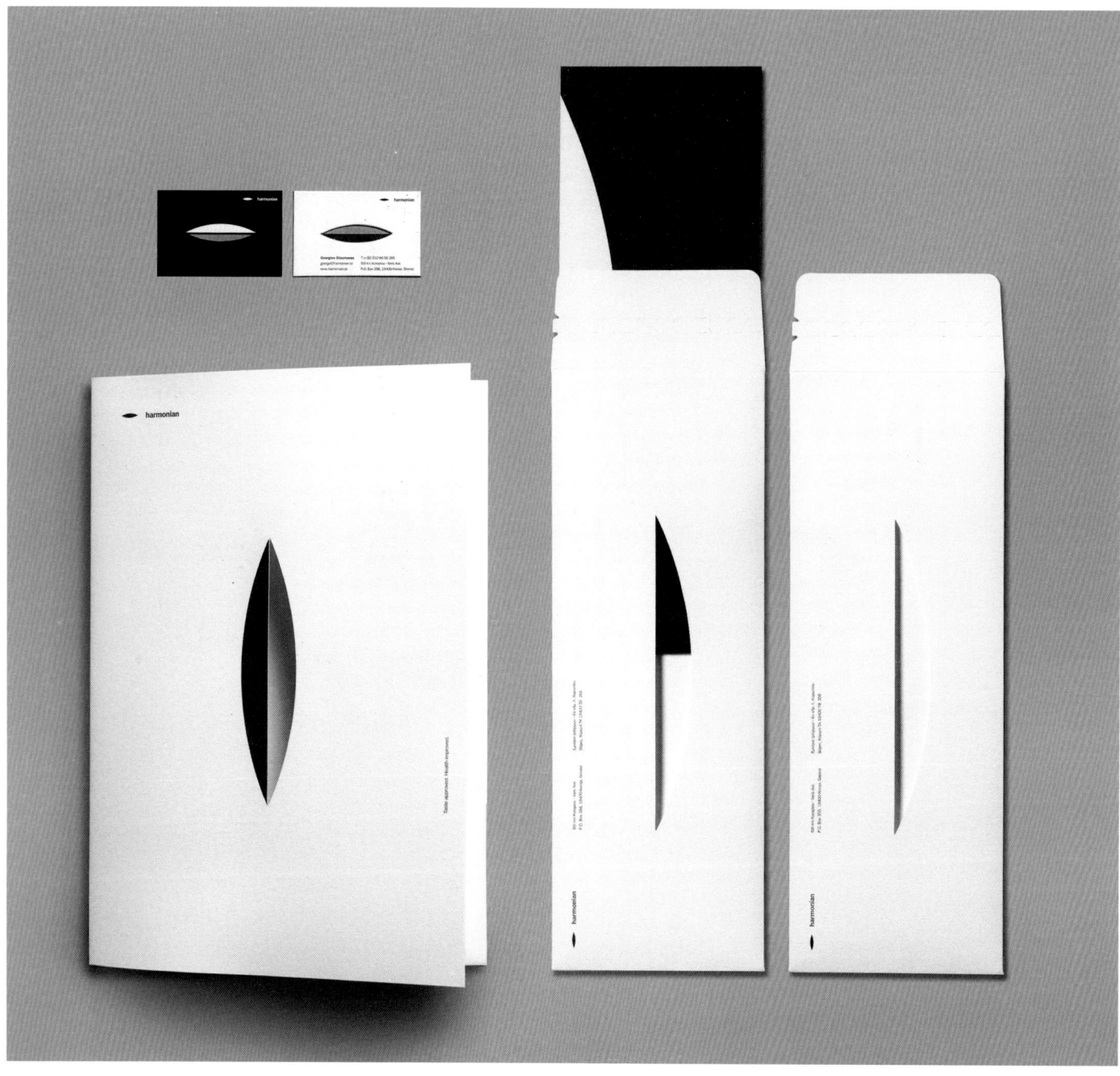

Creative Source from Food

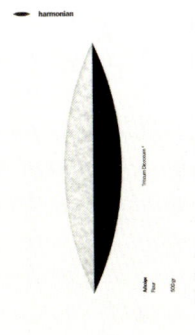
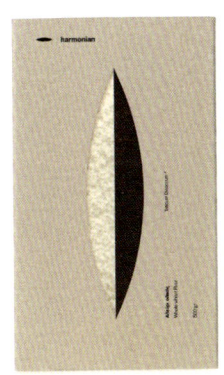

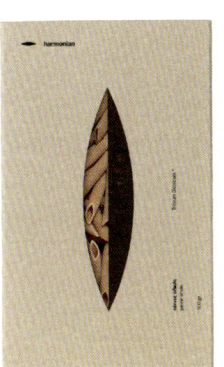

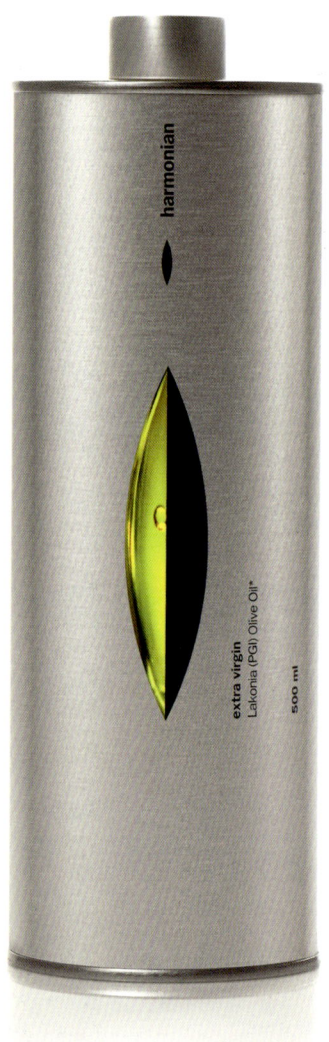

DIALOGUE WITH
Greg

Founder and Creative Director of Mousegraphics Studio. Founded in 1984, Mousegraphics is a well-established creative office and has a considerable expertise in packaging design.

Can you remember what first sparked your interest in design? How old are you when you decided to become a professional designer?

Strangely enough it was the beauty of the designs tools: pencils, pens, compasses, drawing boards, lettering guides, French curves...I was in my early 20's and I was drawn to objects which were elegant and functional in the most essential way.

Did you choose to become a packaging designer or it chose you?

I believe it was the great Picasso who somehow bypassed such dilemmatic questions when he declared, "I do not seek, I find". In my case there was no memorable search process or specific epiphany involved. Neither when I started working in design, nor when Mousegraphics specialized in packaging design, had there been a strategic choice involved. It was rather a meeting of chance and need that decided things.

People often say that you are what we wear, what would you say when it comes to a food package? What does a package mean to a product?

The clothing analogy is an interesting one, in the sense that a person's identity is revealed in clothing; yet it can also be concealed, altered or imagined and this is perfectly ok as far as clothing is concerned. Clothes are animated by people in a way that does not apply to packages where direct display effects are more at play.

For the really short time that it takes for a buying decision to be made, packaging design has to represent the product in every possible way and trigger action on top of desire. This is a different kind of challenge... maybe a package should better somehow undress the product in the eyes of the viewer.

Take olive oil for example, you worked out quite different outfits for a handful of brands. Was the shape of a bottle also a part of your work? (If yes, how to match a bottle to a brand in packaging design?)

As no olive oil is identical to one another, so oil producing companies differ considerably as to how they perceive of themselves, of their product and outlook. We decide on design approaches after we have the whole picture on a project, and we may even suggest something counter to a client's brief and relevant expectations. The choice of a bottle follows the overall design and is determined by it. A rather common glass form can be altered by choices which have to do with texture, the way colour is applied and the materials through which graphics are realised.

All of your works are very concise and directly communicate with the idea of each product. Do you have any criterion when designing new package?

Let's say that we exercise a kind of "informed intuition". Packaging design is a result of a gut feeling as much as a product of an intellectual process shaped by information, negotiation and client input.

Now many products reach customers in various forms, video ad/billboard/packaging/even sounds. Do packaging designers need to cooperate with the relevant video ad designers (like adjusting the graphic design to match the video ad), or it is still comparatively independent?

Packaging design can work with or in another direction from video ads. It all depends on the kind of audiences a company wants to reach and the means it chooses to use. A video commissioned to an artist for a product communication may retain its independence from the product look and still work in its favour. Image consistency is not the holly grail any more especially where smaller brands are concerned. Consumers are more media-educated today and their profiles may differ according to communication channels. There is not one "safe or right" direction in such issues, and as disturbing as this may sound, it is also a quite interesting new reality.

Where do you look for inspiration?

Everywhere. The web and design /art magazines are the obvious sources but they are mostly useful in order to explore developments in the design field and spot possible collaborators; inspiration, i.e. the thing with feathers (to paraphrase Emily Dickinson) is a quite difficult catch and demands complex travels.

Where do you get the name for your studio? Does it have a special meaning for you?

The name was the spontaneous answer to the question about a user name I had to provide real fast. I looked at the computer mouse at the end of my hand and came up with the company name. It is quite unassuming and we gradually grew fond of it.

When you work with foreign clients, is culture difference a big challenge?

Design is a rather fluid universal language, especially now when audiences are also universal and markets much wider.

Our very own company, is a place where diverse cultures and a few nationalities co-exist: Designers specializing in free hand forms, 3D-design or font specialists, Greeks and non Greeks, younger talents and mature professionals, designers with the experience of corporate environments and romantic loners. A client coming from another culture is a challenge we are ready and eager to meet.

When you have different opinions with them, how do you handle with this situation and finally win their trust? (Such as your cooperation with Nongfu Spring, have you ever had any disagreement with each other?)

I think that by now our whole portfolio (works and awards) is providing a context of trust to new clients. We are quite good listeners, ready to get out of our comfort zone, explore and understand in depth the party we work with. In the case of Nongfu, we listened very carefully, we made several proposals (for which we researched the company and the culture it addresses) and we travelled in order to have a first hand experience of the local zeitgeist. Differences of opinion were handled with mutual respect; it was a very interesting and I believe successful cooperation.

Besides your brilliant designers, thanks to your photographer and your press officer, their highly professional work promoted your design to the public. We really want to know how you keep this studio run so effectively.

We are lucky to have a really strong team : top in-house designers, like 2D illustrator specialist Ioanna Papaioannou, as well as famous external collaborators, like photographers Dimitris Poupalos and Tassos Vrettos are only a few of our work partners. Mousegraphics has its own photo studio for product shooting, tests and revisions, as well as the most updated infrastructure and related technical design tools. We are lucky to enjoy a calm and healthy working environment.

As the owner and art director, how do you balance these two different roles? Which one you prefer?

Actually the two roles balance each other in favor of my overall performance. When I obsess with one role, the other provides the necessary resistance.

What's your personal motto?

True is more.

TRUE IS MORE.

BranDirection®

IN MOBILE INTERNET AGE, WHAT IS THE CORE ISSUE FOR CHINESE BRANDS?

Darren Yao, General Manager of Interbrand Shanghai

p.154

THINK POSITIVE, MAKE POSSIBLE

Alex Wilson, Founder & Director of Flamingo Shanghai

p.158

THE STORY OF BRAND PERFECT®

Julie Strawson, Director of Marketing Development, Monotype

p.162

IN MOBILE INTERNET AGE, WHAT IS THE CORE ISSUE FOR CHINESE BRANDS?

Darren Yao

General Manager of Interbrand Shanghai

He is responsible for providing world's leading brand consulting service and developing brand value for clients.

Every industry is facing the subversive challenges from the Internet.

Core Issue One: The construction of brand value is speeding up and therefore we shouldn't hesitate to embrace the age of Internet.

Mobile Internet and digitalization have been widely involved in Chinese brand industry. When talking about them, managers of domestically renowned brands are quite familiar with some hot words such as big data, cloud computing, platform thinking, social media, Mobile Internet and so on.

While being asked whether they have their own digital strategies or not, most of them fail to give a clear answer. Actually they merely follow the herds to do some basic social media communication work. If they couldn't figure out their own strategies of developing brands in mobile-internet age, the future will not be promising.

Core Issue Two: To re-understand the concept of Mobile Internet age while not to be lost in it.

There is a common lack of knowledge of brands as well as digital strategy among Chinese brand clients. For them, brand remains a duty of marketing department which is far from being an essential business and the tasks of digitalization are viewed as merely communicating and advertising instead of a mission shared by all the departments in the entity. What's more common is quite a few enterprises simply consider digitalization as channes of brand communication (online ads, we-chat and micro-blog) or e-commerce plateform. They are more likely to equate digitalization with running e-commerce websites.

Currently there are many key words flooding in the enterprises, such as "customer orientation", "innovation", "openness", "cross-platform", "efficiency", "flexibility", "practice", "progress" and so on, which are pervasive in description of every company's culture.

However when it comes to the perception of these key words, the answers differ from one another. While declaring "customers first" and "sustainable innovation", some of the brand owners are managing their brands in the opposite way, which can be seen in the following cases:

First key words: Customer Orientation
Many brand owners view their priority as "customers first" and believe customer orientation is the characteristic of this era. But the problems are how to inquire about their future needs, whether the needs raised are authentic, if yes how to satisfy them. For example, how to communicate with the customers when he/she considers our price expensive?

The true meaning of customer orientation is neither to wait for being inquired by customers, nor to give whatever they need. It relies on providing true value for customers though in-depth observation,

In Mobile Internet age, what is the core issue for Chinese brands?

exploration of real demands.

Second key word: Innovation
When it comes to the widely discussed topic--"innovation" or "openness", a large amount of brands tend to view it as launching new products, developing new technology terms or creating more modern marketing concepts.

However, actually what we need to think is that whether such innovation is in line with customers' expectations; how to decide the direction of innovation; can the customers perceive our innovation; can it bring higher value for the brand; do the products of innovation require a security from the internal mechanism and process of innovation; and do the ways themselves need innovation too.

Third key words: Market Communication
Now all the brands are aware of the importance of marketing strategy. Lots of them have to spend a lot of money on advertising so as to expand popularity and influences. Social media brought them hopes that with small budget they could win the best result. However later they realised the fact that the Internet media doesn't equal cheap. Actually dramatic changes have occurred to the Internet media as its evolving speed exceeding that of the traditional media both in its quantity and ways of communication. To target specific consumers, money spent on the Internet influential leaders and online water army may even exceed the sum of traditional advertising. Though many brand owners build their official websites, micro-blog and we-chat, and create their own QR code as well as e-commerce platform, but they hardly attract attention from consumers. The feedback of advertisement is becoming more and more sophisticated and unpredictable.

The principle of Marketing communication doesn't change and remains to be who to speak, what to speak and how to speak. What has changed is that the relationship between brands and consumers, as the communication process requires more interaction between them other than being a unilateral one. Both of them are contributors to the brands' value.

Core Issue Three: Brand value construction of traditional industries shows great potential. The authenticity and diversity of brand have been common issues for all walks of life.

Now the competitiveness of traditional industries is no longer mass manufacturing. Brands that are lack of clear visions as well as the ambition to advance are most likely to be weeded out. This requires the owners to explore new ways of brand management and re-build the relationship between brands and consumers. But the common situation is the lack of communication between different departments. Whenever discussing a brand, most people relate it to advertising department and distribution channels or other departments could not provide correspondent brand experience. This leads to a discrepancy in brand experience which severely weakens the authenticity of a brand. In other words a brand does not keep its promise.

At the same time the Internet has been gradually blurred the line between different cities and villages and has assimilated the demands of various group of people. However the uniqueness of a brand is more and more difficult to preserve, which makes it a scarce asset. For example, many e-commercial brands are growing fast with price advantages. But it will be an everlasting topic on how to form their uniqueness and build consumer loyalty.

Most Chinese corporations are not good at price strategy. Brands need to find a niche market and emphasise on product differentiation. They often used price war only proves that they are bad at brand building. The profit of 500 million mobile phones only equal the one of 1 million Apple phones. This huge defence is a result of lack of brand value, and it is the same with beverage, household electrical appliance and automobile.

Many traditional industries envy these emerging new ones which easily earned ten times in the capital market. This reminds us that, the core competitiveness in this era has been transformed from its technology and power to impact on clients and consumers. If we keep exploring the authenticity and uniqueness, brands from traditional industries could also gain abundant profit.

Core Issue Four: What constraint Chinese brands developments are unclear future planning and poor frame of company.

Achievement is not the goal, but the result. Many Chinese brands do not have a clear aim. When we ask those national renowned brands what their brand visions are, the answers are all about sales, achievement or sales volume or to be the top one in industries, in China or even in the globe. And when it comes to the questions what it means to be the so-called top one, what value the brand create for its customers and consumers, there is no one clear answer.

Those outstanding international brands clearly express their brand visions: Apple's perfect combination of humanity and technology, Coca Cola's bringing happiness and joy to people; at the same time they try to fulfil them through delicate and true experience. This endows brands with great vitality as well as a sense of public recognition which leads to continuously good performance.

Many brand owners tend to think that profit comes first and ignore the importance of brand visions. We admit the importance of profit, but without brand visionary there won't be a sustainable development.

The Core Issue in the Future: Chinese brands' key challenge is "lack of imagination".

This is one of the reasons why there appear such a large amount of enterprises expecting instant success without realising the fact that the instant popularity contributed by the Internet doesn't equal to the long-term growth at all.

Many company have troubles in production lines, responsibility of different departments and brand experience, which are due to unclear brand vision. Many medium brands has dozens of SKU, they are similar to each other. The fundamental reason is not only their poor management of production line but also lack of brand vision. Take automobile industry for example, some could compensate their technology disadvantage by taking over foreign brands and gain new sailing points. But it does not help them to build up their own brand. As the price of automobile from foreign and joint venture drops rapidly, those domestic brands would hard to survive simply rely on price advantage.

Without a clear brand vision, the enterprise cannot move on towards a certain direction, not to mention to offer the consistent brand experience. Such a problem needs to be addressed from the very beginning.

The Core Issue in the Future: Chinese brands' key challenge is "lack of imagination".
Some brands are still focusing on making five-year and even ten-year plans. But how could we know the changes in the market and consumers in 5 or 10 years? Whether such plans make sense remains to be seen. Quite a few brand owners fail to give clear answers when asked what they think of the future of the industry. Therefore, what does really make sense is to equip the brands with imagination. To be more specific, to cooperate with the consumers and to create a future that is more promising.

We are not saying a neglect of the importance of executing and brand experience. What we are trying to express is the lack of imagination and an insight into the future, and these may finally lead the brands to lag behind by the times.

Conclusion

The era of Mobile Internet is the best time for Chinese brands to catch up. With more and more problems being revealed, it is essential for them to figure out the relationship between brand and Mobile Internet, otherwise they might lag behind soon. ®

THINK POSITIVE, MAKE POSSIBLE

Alex Wilson

Founder & Director of Flamingo Shanghai
By multiple authors, Chief Editor Alex Wilson

The World of VUCA

The world in which we live in today is so unpredictable, that there are few precedents to gauge the future, and almost anything is possible. VUCA is originally a US military term which has become more commonly adopted to describe the marketing and business to context in which we live: Volatile, Uncertain, Complex and Ambiguous. There are many factors that are radically changing the shape of businesses today, the nature of consumer behaviour and posing challenges in the way brands connect and engage.

First of all, there's a power shift. Brands that have been developed in the West and have largely developed their wealth and reputation in mature markets have for the first time in recent years seen a radical shift in focus, and therefore a need to understand a whole new set of consumers in challenging new environments. Emerging markets are deemed key for growth for the business, resulting in the shift in innovation centres, team structures and the need for new talent around the world. This means re-thinking communication and innovation more than ever.

Secondly, there are new consumer behaviours to confront. When things are uncertain and unpredictable, there is anxiety, and often a lack of trust. No one is suffering more from this than traditional large mainstream corporations, especially in the face of the collaborative consumer. Participation, sharing or simply doing things themselves are routes to greater control and trust. New, nimble, entrepreneurial companies are embracing this change, and are able to cash in by providing solutions for new consumer behaviour.

In this turbulence and flux, the role of brand managers and brand authors become positions of both challenges and opportunities. The role of a brand manager perpetuates the idea of a direct relationship between a brand and the company that seems to control it; one in which every aspect can be controlled, planned and measured. Brand positioning, as a set of values in a presentation, a manifesto on a page, or as layers of an onion in a marketing department model are familiar terms for how we specialise and consider brands. But in a VUCA era, these certainties and models have less meaning, let alone purpose.

So brands are intersections that encompass cultural, geographical, commercial and narrative elements in their breadth. Brands are not owned, they exist as a negotiated space, a conversation between the company, product or service and the consumer and their cultural context. Simply put, a brand is what people think and feel about a product, rather than what they are told.

Brand Authorship

The problem with brand authorship is that it assumes absolute editorial control, a single narrative and denies a sense of ownership to the "recipients". It is the singularity of authorship that feels out of tune with our age. Singularity is losing status in our participative and social-mediated world. Freedom must be given for stories to be created, staged and experienced in a multitude of ways—multiple authors and multiple participants — stories which live, not just stories which

Think Positive, Make Possible

are told. Singularity in authorship leads to exclusivity of ownership, strikingly dissonant with the dominant behaviours of flexing, shaping and adapting to my way, my life and my values. Stories with no role for customers, users or purchasers—are stories to "entertain" not stories to "engage".

The brands that are succeeding are clear on the parameters of their narrative territory and have clarified their brand role. The brand therefore behaves consistently across multiple narratives in the hands of multiple authors. Think Adidas and the way in which they connect their consumers to the heart of adidas and vice versa via the "Adidas Insiders" online community. A digital and social communication platform that is moderated by their global consumer insight team. The platform acts as a liaison among their key target groups and allows them to provide in-depth feedback and explore new ideas on products and the brand that has direct impact on future collections and campaigns.

Open and Living Brands Succeed

Brands that feel "closed" and are in "telling" rather than "living" mode are brands that are clinging to the ideal of authorship. Their flagship communication is a TVC with a beginning, middle and an end. The product is "placed", accessorized and attached to specific lifestyle cues. The engagement model assumes a desire to "copy" rather than to assimilate, adapt and reinterpret. There is only one story. Take it or leave it.

On the flipside, brands who are living, who have momentum, who are open – tend to have the most positive relationships with their customers and the most influence in culture. In a time of vulnerability, uncertainty, complexity and ambiguity – positivity can go a long way. Companies and brands who think positively, can make possible.

Whilst there are many disruptive start-ups who are seizing the opportunities of VUCA, so are larger and more established businesses. IBM and GE are both large global companies whose technology and innovation is more often "behind the scenes" than top of mind for consumers – but both of these brands run fantastic touch-points that help to evangelise how science and technology improves quality of life and makes the world a better place. In doing so, they are setting a discourse for an entire business philosophy, one that is positive and impactful. Importantly, this doesn't happen through advertising slogans or traditional media channels, but a well curated and engaging set of Tumblrs that tie together some of the themes we've mentioned above.

The Tumblr platform allows both brands to invite multiple authors and sources, as both contributors and evangelists. "A Smarter Planet" curated by IBM Global Business Services, has a mission to make the web "instrumented, interconnected and intelligent". The Tumblr curates news and developments in the world of new intelligence, cities, healthcare, education, sustainability and many more. The message is by thinking positively, there are multiple possibilities; and the role for technology is of promise, potential and simplification.

They are companies at the intersection of change and they are transformative businesses who are open to their audiences and the world. "Emoji Science" from GE takes the language of emotions and connections – the Emoji – and transforms it into a tool for education. People are invited to "snap an Emoji, we'll send you some science". Not only is this a playful simplification of the complex world of new technologies, but inspirational to the next generation of thinkers and makers.

Both of these examples demonstrate how, in articulating a brand positioning it is the brand role which therefore becomes the most crucial to define—more important than personality, benefit or values. With a clear brand role there is scope for multiple agency partners, multiple consumers, multiple media channels and multiple experiences with which to weave compelling brand-relevant stories. Multiple authors engaging multiple consumers to build one brand. Brand building for the 21st century.

Brands as Possibilities

Why is this so important now? Where previously we sent the marketing mix into this negotiated space and waited hopefully to see second-order results through sales and share, the mass proliferation of digital and social has allowed us to close the loop. People have always been involved in this dialectic, but now they can be heard. This increases the appetite for brands that are "open", where they can see their own inputs and influence played back. This means that the "positioning" is a start point and a wish-list rather than the end-goal. Rather than feeling like a tightly defined, reductive "thing", we need to aspire to shape brands that have clarity, but at the same time have texture and layers within that clarity, elements clustered round an agreed shared space and meaning. Rather than everything needing exactly the same voice, it now just needs to feel that it is in the same register. This is hugely liberating for brand influencers, it gives us freedom to try new things, to stretch brands at the margins and play at the periphery, as well as offering alternative viewpoints on their core. This means not only engaging in discussion with consumers, but also between different elements of the media plan. Encourage conversation, in the broadest sense, rather than put up a "roadblock"; have your brand ask questions rather than answer them.

To give another example, let's swap from the world of global innovation for something smaller and more local, but equally about the wonder of positivity and potential.

Beast is a local Chinese brand that started in 2011 on Weibo as an online floral service provider. It had no regular SKUs, instead customers came to it with an idea, a personal story, or a description of the gift receiver. Alongside the customer, Beast worked out the name and concept of the floral gift would be like together. At the core of its role and proposition was to create a positive culture among people.

Think Positive, Make Possible

"SIMPLY PUT, A BRAND IS WHAT PEOPLE THINK AND FEEL ABOUT A PRODUCT, RATHER THAN WHAT THEY ARE TOLD."

The novel idea and aspirational aesthetics quickly made Beast popular. It opened an online shop and within one year, it had opened five retail stores in Beijing and Shanghai (including one in Lane Crawford) and two boutique cafes. Its online shop started to incorporate other gift options from a selection of boutique brands. Now the brand also collaborates in multiple formats with artists, celebrities, KOLs via micro-films, zines, training lessons, graffiti and new forms of products.

On a small scale, Beast embodies the opportunities for smart brands in a VUCA era. They understand their audience – young and metropolitan – and they move quickly wherever they go. They don't limit themselves to a category, but proactively extends what it produces, based on the narrative of users.

In summary, VUCA is unsettling, but it's also an exciting time for marketing. But one that requires new leadership skills. When under pressure or threat, it's human nature to want to shut down and protect ourselves, managing our risk rather than embracing the new. And this is where short-term risk and long-term stability play out together. In managing brand behaviour in the short-term, it is the longer-term vision and clarity of the brand role that acts as the anchor, stabilising and providing the parameters for short-term innovation. Remaining open and adaptable in the face of ambiguity, and daring enough to try something new. Our clients are heading in this direction, as agencies we need to ensure we do the same. ®

THE STORY OF BRAND PERFECT®

Julie Strawson

Director of Marketing Development, Monotype

Julie Strawson is a post-graduate qualified member of the Chartered Institute of Marketing, she has spearheaded the conception of brands at Monotype including Fontwise®, Flipfont® and Brand Perfect®.

Something you may be familiar with in brand marketing is the feeling you're taking one step forward and two steps back all the time. The search for campaign perfection is harder than ever to find because of one main culprit: technology. Technology hits us from all angles: from conception through the design process, to implementation and measurement, making it critical that we understand the requirement to maintain brand consistency and authenticity in the eyes of consumers.

In September, The China Internet Network Information Centre (CNNIC)1 reported that Chinese consumers are spending 3.42 hours a day on digital devices and this chart by e-marketer2 shows that digital is consuming almost half US adults' browsing time, so knowing what technology has to offer your brand has never been more critical, especially if your organisation is facing the challenge of working out how to reach customers in new digital channels.

Figure 1: Average time spent per day with major media by US adults. eMarketer, Sept 2014.

Why Brand Perfect?

Considering how dramatically the marketing mix has changed since the introduction of smartphones and other devices it's essential for marketers to understand how to transition their brand across these new channels. Of course this involves design and development teams too, but in founding the Brand Perfect initiative, we wanted to address the technological knowledge gap that exists for many marketers. Brand Perfect is an aspirational brand that strives to discover best practice in digital marketing by sharing knowledge as a community. The ultimate goal is to improve experiences for the consumer and reduce the frustrating cycles that they often have to endure when technology gets in the way. Brand Perfect would address this by providing four key resources to brands: communication, editorially curated information, research, showcase best practice.

Figure 2: The Brand Perfect offering

The search for campaign perfection is harder than ever to find because of one main culprit: technology.

AVERAGE TIME SPENT PER DAY WITH MAJOR MEDIA BY US ADULTS, 2014 *hrs:mins*   Figure 1

Major Media - Total=12hrs 28mins

 Digital **5:46**    TV **4:33**    Radio **1:28**    Print* **0:26**   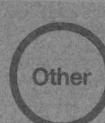 Other **0:14**

Digital

 Desktop/laptop** **2:12**    Mobile (nonvoice) **2:51**   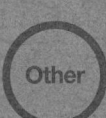 Other **0:43**

Note: ages 18+; time spent with each medium includes all time spent with that medium, regardless of multitasking; for example, 1 hours of multitasking on desktop/laptop while watching TV is counted as 1 hour for TV and 1 hour for desktop/laptop; * includes magazines and newspapers; offline reading only; ** includes all internet activities on desktop and laptop computers
Source: eMarketer, Sep 2014

Figure 2

History Repeats Itself

To understand the way forward it's always helpful to take a look back. Analogous to the internet as a communications vehicle was the mechanisation of printing. At the turn of the 20th century, when books and newspapers were able to be widely mass-produced for the first time, and the reach of communications grew to offer a commercially viable platform for companies to sell products and services. Enter the first large-scale advertising campaigns. People want to be informed and entertained, and here was a new industry set to do that. And the design of new typefaces enabled messages to stand out from body text on the page. Brands such as *The Times* newspaper in London, who understood that typography could help them not only save money on production but also deliver a unique reading experience to build their brand upon, were among the first to invest in designing their own typefaces. Up to the 1950s, the media industry grew with the print industry, the first radio commercial in New York, 1922 and of course television. Advertising entered a new era where actors carried brands forward over the airwaves and on film into the homes of consumers, once again challenging brands to embrace new technology.

Another new specialist industry grew up around it and new standards for type, of secondary importance to this medium, were developed too such as Closed Captioning (CC). Old analogue captions (called CEA-608 captions) displayed only white text on a black background – new platforms need completely new consideration for text support. Of course, with the advent of widely available internet access, the web became the next "big thing" for brand communications, and more than a quarter of a century on, it still is, as it continues to evolve beyond static pages to connect devices and experiences in our everyday lives. This plethora of digital channels now poses a problem to marketers,

Figure 3

In order to plan effectively, brands need data. In order to gather this data, they must look at it holistically by comparing the various channels they are reaching consumers through. Yet, gathering this data using planning and marketing software has been difficult to achieve because there are few industry standards and so many different tools to choose from. Then there is the question of design and execution. When the web came along it brought with it a whole new culture: the digital team, specialists responsible for websites who understood the new tools, technology and the programming languages required to use them. Initially, web standards presented a constrained environment that proved challenging to relay rich brand experiences. This early environment lacked graphics, font choices and colour. As the industry matured, more tools and browsers developed to provide support for images; and a small range of typefaces were made available as system fonts, as was a limited colour palette.

A key cultural shift in consumer behaviour that has made brands sit up and take notice is the move to mobile. Mobile phones have played a valuable role in the developing world, with opportunities from micropayment banking driving app development in the financial services sector, for instance, while in the West, mass adoption of smartphones has seen brands begin to seriously invest in reaching consumers via mobile, and make mobile a key part of their marketing strategies.

Figure 3: Brand Perfect's launch campaign

The Broken Brand

The early days of mobile posed significant challenges to brands. I had a conversation in 2010 with the brand guardian of a global bank. He explained how he had invested years building a distinct brand identity

A key cultural shift in consumer behaviour that has made brands sit up and take notice is the move to mobile.

complete with a unique typeface only to find that the bank's digital team wasn't using it. He showed me their first mobile app. It bore no aesthetic resemblance to the brand, and due to this he doubted that anyone would use the app because they would not be able to trust that it was a genuine product. Back then mobile user interfaces had limited support for rich graphics and there was no choice in typefaces. That was when I stumbled across the first issue in the path to brand perfection – how does one create consistent brand experiences that flow across all customer touch-points? From his experience it was clear that there was little co-operation happening between the digital and brand marketing teams. This raised a second issue – the need for collaboration between business, design and development teams responsible for a brand. We were starting to get to the root of the problem. Yet, there was the ongoing challenge of how to stay informed about consumer technology trends to help design the brand strategy going forward. Unlike printing a campaign, digital platforms were not delivered with type built in. In digital, it was proving far from easy to deliver engaging, authentic brand communications.

Enter Brand Perfect by Monotype

After this research project was complete, it was clear that we had a specific need and some very broad issues that had to be addressed. Instead of being purely about type, the Brand Perfect initiative would harness all the experience Monotype had gained working with brands regardless of the technology to deliver beautiful readable brand experiences. And the Brand Perfect initiative's remit would not just be to report on that process but would actually attempt to showcase state-of-the-art technology and design into the experience delivered. ®

This raised a second issue – the need for collaboration between business, design and development teams responsible for a brand.

BranDream®

The Spirit of Hong Kong : Ambition and Creation

Editor: Lisha Xie

Every designer may have a dream to establish his/her own brand, but there doubtlessly is no easy way to go. Some designers might have no idea where to start, some might be right in trouble and do not know how to move on. This time our brand new column starts our journey to design from the first stop Hong Kong. In this cosmopolis known for ambition and creation, by interviewing various talents from prominent Hong Kong image stylist Tina, to emerging fashion designer Rose and Polly, to former copy writer Andrew in creative cultural industry, we bring their stories right in front of you and hope to bring you some inspirations.

Tina's Choice
PASSION FORGING YOUR DREAM

Ibility
CROCHETING THE FAMILY DREAM

Loom Loop
MIXING UP TRADITION WITH INNOVATION

Mall 852
BRANDING HONG KONG CULTURE

Tina's Choice

PASSION FORGING YOUR DREAM

Tina Liu
Tina's Choice CEO / Prominent Image Stylist of Hong Kong

———

Once we mentioned Tina, many may associate the name with various titles, actresses, singers, hosts or directors, and of course the most impressive one image stylist, with honorary name such as "Image Guru" and "The Chief Image Consultant of China". When we brought many designers' problems with us and tried to start this interview with a pleasantry about her recent work, she broke in "If we are discussing design, let's focus on it and save all those entertainment reporter's opening speech!" obviously revealing her serious attitude toward this interview. Whenever we asked a question highly concerned by designers, she often raised her head in meditation and gave her opinion wisely; when we described designers' inner doubts, she would stop me with her answer. This is Tina, the CEO of Tina's Choice select shop. From a whole new point of view, we hope you will be inspired by this short interview by opening up this fabulous life book of Tina and extracting her understanding of brand and design.

TINA'S CHOICE NOW HAVE AROUND FIFTY ACCESSORY BRANDS, AND DESIGNERS FROM EACH BRAND HAVE QUITE DIFFERENT STYLES. FROM YOUR POINT OF VIEW, WHAT IS THE MOST IMPORTANT THING BEING A DESIGNER?

Passion! I know it seems like an ordinary answer but it is true! There is no easy way to become a successful designer. If you were an artist, you are expressing yourself and it would be ok to shut yourself off. But if you are a designer, you are communicating with many people. You have to consider what you want to express, and whether people will understand or like it. Once you launch your product in the market, you are supposed to think over many aspects. All of these will lead to a series of problems which you need to solve. If you do not have enough passion, it is really a no easy way to go.

WE FOUND THAT MANY DESIGNERS ARE PASSIONATE ABOUT THEIR WORK, BUT SOME OF THEM ARE MERELY CONSIDERED AS CRAFTSMEN. WHEN THEY WANT TO STEP FURTHER AND ESTABLISH THEIR OWN BRAND TO GAIN MORE RECOGNITIONS, WHAT SHOULD THEY DO?

(Pondering) Actually design is similar to other professions. You need to have your uniqueness. Either you are fashion designer, product designer, graphic designer or interior designer, ask yourself what the value and characteristic of your design are? Did you dedicate yourself to your works? If you think your works best represent your talent, how to present it and let other people remember, in other words, how to market it. Think about where the demand is. Some products might be easy to be accepted, some might take a comparatively long time to find specific target consumers.

What is brand? I think we have to figure this out first; brand is not the ultimate goal. You tell me what is brand. Are we going to finish 99 projects to build a brand, or are we committed ourselves to a career, and later it becomes our brand? This two sequences will make a huge difference.

DO YOU BELIEVE THE LATTER ONE OFTEN MAKES DESIGNERS MORE PASSIONATE AND DEDICATED?

Where did those Time-honoured brands come from? I always believe that every product starts from a basic concept, take a knife for example, a knife maker might simply want to create the best knife and he makes a living on it. Gradually his products are well-known for their quality and reasonable prices, then his name becomes a promise to his products. A brand does not come out from thin air. Now we see that many businessmen put the cart before the horse.

DO YOU THINK THAT'S WHY MANY DESIGNERS FAILED TO BUILD A WELL-ESTABLISHED BRAND?

There are many reasons and this is one of them. Some designers lack perseverance, some lack talent, while some have both but did not have the chance. I said passion is an essential element because you are facing problems all the time and you might not solve all of them. A famous Chinese saying is that a general builds his success on ten thousand bleaching bones, you have to understand that those glamorous brands were survived from a fierce competition.

AS A FOUNDER OF A SELECT SHOP, MANY DESIGNERS WANT TO KNOW WHAT YOUR CONSIDERATION IS WHEN YOU MAKE YOUR CHOICE.

Balance sensibility and rationality. As a select shop owner, trends, my favour, price and market demand are all I need to think over. If you want to become a good buyer, you have to balance your personal preference with object factors. Like a housewife, she has to use limited budget to create a marvellous feast, not only taste good but is sufficient for everybody. She needs to know what her family like and what her guests like. A buyer is the same, he/she has to think over and over again. It would never be as simple as buying a Christmas gift for your friends.

Now we have dozens of brands, those were selected from hundreds. A mature designer should understand that a buyer did not choose your products because he/she have a comprehensive consideration. Don't be frustrated. On the other hand, designers need to know this environment. Of course big order would be a reward to them, but no order does not means your product or your design is not good.

THIS MIGHT LEAD TO ANOTHER QUESTION, MANY DESIGNERS MIGHT BE CONFIDENT WITH THEIR WORKS, BUT AFTER BEING TURNED DOWN FOR MANY TIMES, THIS DEFINITELY WILL WEAKEN THEIR RESOLVE. (SOME MAY SACRIFICE THEIR ORIGINAL IDEA.)

They will never forget! I know what you want to ask! Will those designers surrender to reality? I think this depends on designers, some of them, either fashion designer, furniture designer or shoe designer, can alter or improve their idea and continue to express themselves. I would say this is positive and this is not failure. Whether you will get recognised or not, you have the right to stick to your idea, but the responds might still be negative. Or maybe it would take a long time for you to find your target consumer, they might be in another country.

HAVE YOU EVER THOUGHT ABOUT MAKING YOUR OWN PRODUCT FROM SCRATCH? WHAT'S YOUR BLUEPRINT FOR TINA'S CHOICE?

I did not design a product, but I mainly do the editing, how to match different elements. Such as my bracelet named *Roman Holiday* successfully released in the market. In 2015 I will launch my new products all designed by ourselves. I hope in the future whenever people mention Tina's Choice, they will connect it with uniqueness, good looking but not expensive. Many people praised my styling, but I hope my product could convey my idea. People do not need to invite me to a lot of places, when they see my selection and product, they will understand my concept behind design.

Ibility

CROCHETING THE FAMILY DREAM

Rose Lee / Peter Lin
Creative Director / Director

———

With the passion and love for handcraft crochet, several young people gathered together to realise a family dream by crocheting their own brand. When creative director Rose stood in front of us, we were surprised by the determination revealed from her gentle voice; when Manager Peter answered our question calmly but firmly, we learned the brand's continuous growth. From these two main founders of Ibility, let's find out how they turned their dream into reality.

IBILITY IS PROUD OF ITS HAND CRAFTED CROCHET, WE ALL KNOW THAT HANDCRAFT IS REALLY TIME-CONSUMING AND HIGH-COST, WHY DO YOU ATTACH SO MUCH IMPORTANCE ON THIS?

Peter: That's part of the reason why we establish this brand. Actually Rose is deeply influenced by her mother and great-grandfather, who were very passionate about crochet and hand craft. Her mother sacrificed her design career to this family. So Rose inherits this love for crochet and hope to incorporate different techniques of crochets to our fashion design. Crochet is our brand DNA. Our name derived from three words: possibility, ability and sensibility. We hope it is the same with the future of crochet, it could mix various elements and bring new possibilities.

Rose: We want to promote this handicraft art and culture, and hope it won't be lost. I think it is our responsibility to advocate the importance of handicrafts, sure this will also elevate our brand value. This is very common in handmade bags and watches.

HOW DO YOU IDENTIFY YOUR TARGET MARKET? IS IT A GOOD STRATEGY TO DEVELOP A MULTIPLE PRODUCTION LINE FROM BABY TO WOMAN CLOTHING FOR A NEW BRAND?

Peter: Considering our production cost, our target consumers are middle class who appreciate hand crafted crochet and green fashion. We hope to preserve these hand craft skills and at the same time bring out great design. We chose to develop a rich fashion collection mainly because this will contribute to our development. If we focus on baby collection, the market share will definitely shrink. But woman's clothing will help us expand the market.

Rose: Also we noticed that now many young mothers are very fashionable. They would love their baby to have a similar style with them.

ROSE, NOW YOU ARE BOTH THE CREATIVE DIRECTOR AND BRAND FOUNDER, HOW DO YOU BALANCE THE TWO DIFFERENT ROLES?

Rose: I am very happy to have our own brand. Of course now we have much more problems and difficulties than ever before. I have to always put the production cost in mind, trying to apply crochet in various fabrics in order to avoid monotony. We need to enrich our collection to make sure they will reach those young customers. I would say to stay fashionable and keep our brand features are very important.

HAVE YOU EVER MET ANY DIFFICULTY? HAVE YOU EVER THOUGHT ABOUT GIVING UP?

Peter: We had been through a difficult time, facing problems both in marketing and production. After all our brand is only 2 years old. It is too hard for us to find the right workers at the beginning. We hope our company has a responsibility to this society, so you will find that most of our employees came from mainland (who need a job to make a living) or some middle-aged women, we hope to offer a job to them. Meanwhile we provide opportunities to those potential young designers who have their dreams. So we have a good team, all of us are passionate about our work.

Rose: Never give up. A good team is essential. We are so lucky to have them and our partner together with us to face all troubles. We are all dedicated to this brand, so never give up.

COULD YOU GIVE A PIECE OF ADVICE FOR THOSE YOUNG DESIGNERS WHO HAVE THEIR OWN DREAMS?

Peter: Broaden your horizon and persevere to the end. It is necessary to observe the world around you. Now many designers have brilliant ideas and concepts, but sometimes they are too isolated. It seems all design comes from computers.

Rose: I am obsessed with crochet and I often go to different places and expose myself to exhibition, emerging myself to different culture and history. I also study how many techniques and skills of crochet in the world. Now my employees and I often discuss new skills, we even invent new crochet hook.

WHAT'S YOUR BLUEPRINT FOR IBILITY?

Hope we could have our flagship shops in Beijing and Shanghai. We are now already on the way.

Loom Loop

MIXING UP TRADITION WITH INNOVATION

Polly Ho / Andy Wong
Design Consultant / Chief Designer & Director

Having engaged in the design industry for more than decades, these two well experienced designers, gregarious and outgoing Polly together with steady and wise Andy, founded a sustainable fashion brand Loom Loop.

WHERE DOES YOUR NAME LOOM LOOP COME FROM?

We had a brainstorm and have our English name first. We wanted to start from the basic elements and loom refers to the machine which produces cloth. Every piece of cloth was woven together those loops. Also this name represents us, the two founders. We also considered the graphic design, which perfectly matches each other. So we chose Loom Loop. The Chinese name, both two words have the same pronunciation. The first "Lu" means normal and busyness, while the second "Lu" means wealth. We hope our design could bring people rich and wealth, and our busy work and effort could bring us luck and honour.

MANY OF YOUR CLOTHES ARE MADE OF 100% SILK, WILL THIS CONSTRAIN YOUR DESIGN CONCEPT? HOW TO EXPRESS YOUR BRAND CHARACTERISTICS BESIDES MATERIAL?

As each kind of material has its own strength, we often develop our idea after we receive a piece of cloth. Maybe some of our materials are not suitable for exaggerated design, but we have to keep our style. We want our collections easy to match, comfortable to wear and timeless. We have three main features. Firstly, 100% original. Each of our collections has a theme and all patterns are designed by ourselves. Secondly, we want to combine Chinese culture with western culture, because both of us were born in HK and had studied and worked in the UK. Thirdly we have a concern about sustainable fashion. We will choose suppliers who use eco-friendly printing and organic cotton. At the same time, we also dedicate to recycle those leftover clothes.

Mixing up Tradition with Innovation

NOW AS A DESIGNER AND FOUNDER OF LOOM LOOP, WHAT IS THE BIGGEST DIFFERENCE COMPARING WITH YOUR PREVIOUS WORK?

I think the attitude and mentality have changed a lot. Now I have to think about many things. In my previous job maybe I need to satisfy my boss and customers' needs, but now I have more freedom to express my idea. I do not want to pay too much attention on making money. Creating something you like and others appreciate, that makes me happy. I know it is really hard, but I do enjoy my work now.

FOR THOSE DESIGNERS WHO HAVE THEIR OWN DREAMS, DO YOU HAVE ANY PIECE OF ADVICE?

Every entrepreneur might have their own way to start up his business. We started our brand after we know the PMQ programme and opened our first shop. When we do not have enough employees, this shop along has driven us crazy. We may not have time to do the promotion and marketing. I would advise some designers do not hurry up to open a shop or work studio, because this will take a lot of your money and time. Your marketing and new collection developing might lag behind.

WHAT'S YOUR BLUEPRINT FOR LOOM LOOP?

Every designer want to have their own brand. Polly and I hope this brand will be our lifelong career, and gradually makes an impact on people. As for the market, it is not limited to HK. We will enter Mainland firstly, and step by step to Milan, London and Paris.

Mixing up Tradition with Innovation

Mall 852

BRANDING HONG KONG CULTURE

Andrew Au yeung
Founder and Director

———

He went abroad at the age of 15, but later chose to come back to Hong Kong after his whole family immigrated to Canada. He majored in Journalism, but has been working in advertising agency for decades. With the passion for Hong Kong culture, now he has a new title—the founder of gift & premium shop Mall 852. His name is Andrew, who will introduce us how to build a brand from local cultural heritage.

YOU MAJORED IN JOURNALISM, WHY DO YOU CHANGE YOUR CAREER TO DESIGN INDUSTRY?

Qualification is not a must for a designer. Creation starts with the concept behind it. When I worked in my first advertising agency, I had a lot of chances to take part in every process and learned a lot from there. In advertising agencies, there are two important roles, copy writer and art director, and I prefer the former. I often shared my idea with different art directors and received their responds, this is a good way to enrich my knowledge. Gradually I went toward my own understanding of design. For me, my work is to know each designer's strength and inspire them to realise my concept.

WHY DO YOU ESTABLISH THIS BRAND AT THE BEGINNING? AFTER SEVERAL YEARS' DEVELOPMENT, IS THERE ANY CHANGE IN YOUR BUSINESS POLICY?

We hope to advocate the history and culture of HK, but this is not necessarily limited to history book or documentary film. It could be a product or a T-shirt. So we develop our products from unique HK culture. There is no big changes in business policy. Every brand has its core value and its DNA. We have a meeting annually in which we look over all our works to see whether we deviate from our original path.

COULD YOU GIVE US A BRIEF INTRODUCTION OF YOUR TEAM AND YOUR MANAGEMENT?

We have a full time designer and partners. Now we collaborate with many designers to develop new products. You know every designer has a different style from each other and this helps us to enrich our collection. My job is to find designers who can help us to finish our work. Besides I also cooperate with other agencies, helping them to design and launch new products. This also supports our own design business.

WHAT ARE THE DIFFERENCES BETWEEN BEING AN EMPLOYEE AND A LEADER OF YOUR OWN COMPANY?

We tend to think the grass is greener on the other side. If I had been in my previous work, I might have a comparatively wealthy living. But you also have problems, such as cut down by the boss. Especially when you hold a high position, you have to deal with too much bureaucracy. That's not what I like. I think you have to know yourself very well. Some people have the ability, but they might be good employees instead of leaders, because they do not have perseverance facing difficulties. When you become a leader of your company, you have to take care of too many things and be prepared for any problem and go ahead. I would say it is important to know what type of person you are.

BRANDISCOVERY®

ORIGI-NALITY/CUL-TURE/EVENTS

ORIGINALITY

SUPERHERO

As American superhero comics are popular throughout the world, the film industry also owns their profit and fame with the superheroes like Iron Man, Captain America, etc. The following info-graphic manifests that Marvel and DC, the two comic tycoons are definitely the winners with the help of these superheroes.

Red Bull Superheroes

The Red Bull Superheroes Project depicts a playful union between the Austrian energy drink and the Justice League University. This design is inspired by the uniforms of superheroes from various ages of the comic books. By using a mix of techniques, including vector illustrations and 3D renders, the project took four months for Diego Fonseca to complete.

Diego Fonseca ° 2014

ORIGINALITY

BranDiscovery®

RESOURCEFUL

AGILE

VERSATILE

CLASSIC

ADVANCED

MFA Superhero Brand Connections

A logo can be one of a hero's most defining assets. While not an all-inclusive representation of the brand, its symbol—an icon of strength, justice and hope—resonates with the audience. A brand, just like a superhero, lives and breathes. Although represented visually by a single mark, a brand's essence is truly defined and comes to life through a brand's actions.

MFA Superhero Brand Connections explored elements of design using a constructed analogy of superheroes. These elements, primarily the use of symbol, colour and typography, have the power to communicate with an audience far beyond the surface level.

Matthew G. Olin ° M@OH!

Christopher Reeve Photo Shoot

Chistopher Reeve is "the hero" that Cihan Ünalan grew up with and his portrayal of Superman had a very dramatic effect on him as a child. This was such a strong inspiration for him that movies and fantastic world of heroes have become the source of inspiration. Feeling so strongly about the subject, Cihan Ünalan wanted to create a tribute series in his honour.

Christopher Reeve Photo Shoot ° Atilla Karabay & Cihan Ünalan

Heroes of Our Generation

Compelled by the reality of bullying, Adriana Arciniegas has started the project Heroes of Our Generation, a series of oil paintings and art installations that give voice to the victims of bullying and those who are taking a stand against it. Painted realistically as superheroes, these children are an example to society for speaking out about their bullying experiences as an effort to encourage children, teenager and adults to take a stand alongside them and combat this pandemic social scourge.

Heroes of Our Generation ° Adriana Arciniegas

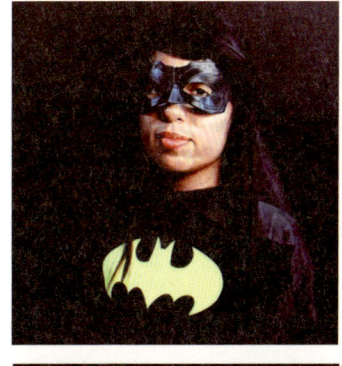

EVENTS

25/ 1 - 29/ 3

CALL FOR ENTRIES 2015 & BLOOM PROJECTS

Exhibition Date: January 25 to March 29, 2015
Exhibition Place: Museum of Contemporary Art Santa Barbara

Museum of Contemporary Art Santa Barbara (MCASB) will present Call For Entries 2015 & Bloom Projects during January 25 to March 29, 2015. In a range of artistic mediums that include performance, painting, social practice, and sculpture, this highly anticipated 8th annual exhibition reveals the vibrancy, creativity, and innovative thinking present in local area. Also on view is new and recent work by Los Angeles-based artist Conrad Ruiz in the next iteration of the cutting-edge Bloom Projects series.

www.mcasantabarbara.org

27/ 2

iF DESIGN AWARD 2015

Award Ceremony Date: February 27, 2015

The iF DESIGN AWARD 2015 will be given to winners instead of the traditional individual brands (iF product design award, iF communication design award and iF packaging design award) from the 2015 season, aiming to acknowledge the close interconnections between the different design disciplines. Being focused on one single brand, it is believed that the award will further strengthen its role as a seal of quality for excellent design and lead to more communicative impact.

The iF DESIGN AWARD 2015 features the following disciplines: Product, Communication, Packaging, Interior Architecture and Professional Concept. The jury meeting will be held from January 20 to 22, 2015, and the award ceremony, the iF design night, will take place on February 27, 2015.

www.ifdesign.de

13/ 3 - 16/ 3

INTERNATIONAL FURNITURE FAIR SINGAPORE

Exhibition Date: March 13 to 16, 2015
Exhibition Place: Singapore EXPO

The International Furniture Fair Singapore, held in conjunction with the ASEAN Furniture Show (IFFS/AFS), the Décor Show and the Hospitality 360°, is regarded by industry experts as Asia's premier sourcing platform and design-led exhibition. Returning to Singapore EXPO from March 13 to 16, 2015, the trilogy of design-led events will occupy interconnected Halls 1 through 6 and feature a comprehensive range of furniture, furnishing, decorative accessories, interiors and fittings by a diverse portfolio of quality exhibitors. The show's primary objective is to facilitate conversations and create business opportunities between manufacturers and designers, distributors, retailers, and hoteliers.

www.IFFS.com.sg

Events

9TH INTERNATIONAL ARTE LAGUNA PRIZE

Final Exhibition Date: March, 2015
Exhibition Place: Arsenale of Venice

The Italian Cultural Association MoCA (Modern Contemporary Art), in collaboration with Arte Laguna Studio, organises the 9th Edition of the International Arte Laguna Prize, aimed at promoting and enhancing Contemporary Art. Its selection procedure will last from December, 2014 to January, 2015, the selected entries will be announced in February, and the final exhibition will be held in Arsenale of Venice in March.

www.artelagunaprize.com

DESIGN SHANGHAI 2015

Exhibition Date: March 27 to 30, 2015
Exhibition Place: Shanghai Exhibition Centre

The second edition of Design Shanghai 2015 will take place from March 27 to 30, 2015, at Shanghai Exhibition Centre. This show will feature more than 300 exhibitors across three halls: Contemporary Design, Classic Design and Collectible Design. Among the confirmed installations, Bally's Jean Prouvé 6x9 house will become the focal point.

www.designshowshanghai.com

RED DOT AWARD: PRODUCT DESIGN 2015

Winner's exhibition Date: June 30 to July 26, 2015
Exhibition Place: Red Dot Design Museum Essen

The Red Dot Award: Product Design 2015 is calling for entries to global brands and established names in the world of design, but equally to small and medium-sized companies and young talents. The regular registration period is from December 6, 2014 to January 27, 2015 and the latecomers are available until February 11, 2015. Young designers can apply for free registrations on December 10, 2014. Jury Session will be held in February and all winners will be honoured at the Red Dot Gala in the Aalto Theater in Essen on June 29. From June 30 to July 26, the winner's exhibition "Design on Stage" opens in the Red Dot Design Museum Essen.

www.red-dot.org/pd

CULTURE

《北欧のかわいい紙雑貨とペーパーデコ・レシピ》

Publisher°	Graphic-sha
ISBN°	9784766127126
Softcover°	144 pages
Language°	Japanese
Product Dimensions°	182×146 mm

Introduction: This book introduces decorative styles of living rooms, arrangements of family parties, and handmade adornments and menus in Northern Europe. These adornments made of paper are not only environmental but also creative. You can decorate your own room and living room according to the style you want, and adorn parties with handmade decorations. Dishes made by mothers are the most delicious food in the world, so you can enjoy this wonderful food in Northern Europe in this book.

《北欧スウェーデン 暮らしの中のかわいい民芸》

Publisher°	PIE
ISBN°	9784756245144
Softcover°	175 pages
Language°	Japanese
Product Dimensions°	210×148 mm

Introduction: Surrounded by the dense forest, Sweden has especially long winters. In Northern Europe, the culture of household handicrafts is nurtured by nature. Folk arts and crafts, such as paintings on the wooden horses and baskets made of branches of birches, are passed down through the ages. This book features folk arts and crafts existing in Northern Europe.

《羊毛フェルトでつくる小鳥のブローチ》

Publisher°	Graphic-sha
ISBN°	9784766126907
Softcover°	80 pages
Language°	Japanese
Product Dimensions°	208×140 mm

Introduction: This book introduces works of Chikusa, a popular hand-maker in woolen world. There are lovely birds, trees, fruit, flowers, and some breastpins made of wool. This book detailedly presents the process of making woolen works, so you will find no difficulties during the learning process even if you are just a beginner.

《The Design of IIDA KASATEN IIDA》

Publisher°	PIE
ISBN°	9784756244819
Softcover°	128 pages
Language°	Japanese
Product Dimensions°	210×148 mm

Introduction: IIDA is a brand of umbrella in Japan. Members in IIDA use fabrics, handles and ribs to make their own umbrellas. This book features how these umbrellas are made, stories behind the umbrellas and IIDA's latest works. Lots of fabrics hobbyists are attracted by the delicate patterns on the umbrellas as well as product designers are enlightened by IIDA's concept contained in the craftwork.